D1083295

A FIELD GUIDE TO THE WARBLERS OF BRITAIN AND EUROPE

A FIELD GUIDE TO THE WARBLERS OF BRITAIN AND EUROPE

BY ALICK MOORE

ILLUSTRATED BY BRYON WRIGHT

OXFORD UNIVERSITY PRESS · 1983

Oxford University Press, Walton Street, Oxford OX2 6DP

London Glasgow New York Toronto
Delhi Bombay Calcutta Madras Karachi
Kuala Lumpur Singapore Hong Kong Tokyo
Nairobi Dar es Salaam Cape Town
Melbourne Auckland

and associates in
Beirut Berlin Ibadan Mexico City Nicosia

Published in the United States
by Oxford University Press, New York

© *Text: Alick Moore; illustrations: Bryon Wright, 1983*

British Library Cataloguing in Publication Data
Moore, Alick
A field guide to the warblers of Britain
and Europe.
1. Passeriformes—Identification   2. Birds
—Europe—Identification
I. Title
598.8'094   QL696.P2
ISBN 0–19–217710–9

Library of Congress Cataloging in Publication Data
Moore, Alick.
A field guide to the warblers of Britain and Europe.

Bibliography: p.
Includes index.
1. Wood warblers—Identification. 2. Birds—
Identification. 3. Birds—Great Britain—
Identification. 4. Birds—Europe—Identification.
I. Title.
QL696.P279M66   1983   *598.8'43'094   83–11456*
ISBN 0–19–217710–9

Printed in Hong Kong

Contents

Plates

(Plates fall between pp. 82 and 83 of the text)

NOTE ON MAPS

Where no map is provided the bird does not breed anywhere within the indicated area, and enters it only as a vagrant or accidental visitor.

Introduction

The Old World Warblers constitute the subfamily Sylviinae, an important section of the large passerine family Muscicapidae which includes Thrushes, Flycatchers, and many others. They should be clearly separated from the New World Warblers or Wood Warblers (Parulidae) which are confined to the American continent and have only nine primary wing feathers as opposed to the ten of the Sylviinae.

The Sylviinae comprises about 305 species distributed throughout the Old World from Europe and Asia to Africa and Australasia. Thirty-nine species breed in Europe, but the whole list for Europe including accidentals and vagrants amounts to about 55 species.

Warblers are generally small or very small in size; are mostly plainly coloured, usually shades of green, brown, and grey. They have fine, narrow, pointed bills and are mostly (in Europe) arboreal and insectivorous. In most of the genera the sexes are similar and they differ from Thrushes and Flycatchers in having an unspotted immature plumage resembling the adult plumage. Some species of Warbler resemble each other very closely so that precise identification may be an expert matter, using as specific characteristics small structural differences such as relative length and shape of primary wing feathers. In many cases, field identification is made easier by striking differences in the songs which are frequently varied and melodious.

Warblers may inhabit trees, shrubs, reeds, or grass. They are highly active, searching ceaselessly for small insects, spiders, eggs, and larvae. Some may add fruit and berries to their diets in late summer. They live mostly solitarily or in pairs, the males usually having striking territorial songs.

Nests are placed in thick foliage, or attached to reed stems or placed on or near the ground. They may be open, cup-shaped, purse-shaped, or domed with a side entrance. Eggs of European warblers normally number

4–6, and are incubated by the female only or by the female and the male, and both sexes feed the fledgelings.

In view of the mainly insect diet, warblers living in cold or temperate regions are highly migratory, the majority of European warblers wintering in north or tropical Africa. In addition to a post-nuptial moult, often not started until reaching winter quarters, many species have a pre-nuptial moult.

This book omits one or two extreme fringe species and covers 53 species likely to be encountered in the west Palaearctic area.

THE IMPORTANCE AND DISCIPLINE OF IDENTIFICATION

All knowledge of these birds is based on correct identification. I have sometimes watched a warbler being identified by bird watchers with immediate and facile authority based on the scantiest sightings, and on such flimsy bases many of these 'identifications' go forward as serious records. The principal purpose of this book is to make the identification of warblers easier to approach and to provide some bases on which to make sound diagnoses.

Warblers represent some of the greatest challenges to the bird watcher in Europe. Not only are the differences between species very slight, but the views offered to the watcher are frequently brief and unsatisfactory; the bird may give a series of impressions before any clear feature is seen, and much time and patience may be needed before a certain identification is made.

In attempting to provide a review of these features I have assumed that the watcher is examining the bird in the field and has not got it in the hand. Specialized literature exists to explain fully the use of wing formulae in making precise identifications, but the opportunities to examine birds in the hand are few and most diagnoses must be made from the sights and sounds of birds in the field. Warbler identification brings into action every facet of the bird's appearance, activity, voice, and habitat and many birds require a detailed report on all these characters.

There is no short cut. It is generally pointless to stalk

most of these warblers and even less rewarding to try to frighten them or beat them out of their hiding places. A great deal more knowledge will be gained by remaining at a distance, quite still and quiet, and observing what the bird allows while it is unaware of the watcher's presence. Patience is everything.

It may be helpful to use these comments and questions as an identification checklist of features which I have adapted to cover some of the problems encountered when watching warblers. Assuming that the bird is silent and only giving fleeting opportunities to watch it, the following may be considered.

General first impression	Any obvious or distinctive features in plumage, shape, behaviour. General colouring.
Body	Contrasts in colour between head, back, rump, tail and between throat, breast, flanks, and belly. (It may be helpful to alter the background and light angle to check these.)
Tail	Relatively long or short? Any white in it? Rounded, square-ended, graduated? Undertail coverts. How long? Colour contrast with belly? With tail feathers? Is tail flicked, cocked, or opened?
Wings	Wingbars? How many? How wide, long, and clear? Rounded or pointed wings? How are they held at rest? Do they droop?
Head	Shape. General roundness, or flatness of forehead? Crown stripe? Supercilium? Length, breadth, colour? Do they meet on nape or forehead? Eye and eye ring colour?
Legs	Colour?
Bill	Length? Strong or weak-looking? Colour and difference between upper and lower mandibles?

Mouth	Colour of gape if bird is calling or singing?
Behaviour	Dainty or clumsy in movements? Hovering? Feeding station. Ground, low vegetation or higher? What is the bird doing, why and how is it doing it?
Note	It is very important to be consistent in your interpretation of plumage colours. If you write down, or have in your mind the colour 'olive', do you mean greenish-olive, brownish-olive, or another dominant shade? It may be helpful to practise setting standards for yourself by re-examining very familiar birds such as Robin, Blackbird, Song Thrush, etc., and naming variations of their colours consistently. What I call, for instance, greyish-brown may have quite a different interpretation in your mind.

Species

Order is that of Dr K. H. Voous in *List of recent Holarctic bird species*, 1977, *Ibis* 119.

Cettia cetti (Temminck) — Cetti's Warbler
Cisticola juncidis (Rafinesque) — Fan-tailed Warbler
Prinia gracilis (M. H. C. Lichtenstein) — Graceful Warbler
Scotocerca inquieta (Cretzschmar) — Scrub Warbler
Locustella certhiola (Pallas) — Pallas' Grasshopper Warbler
Locustella lanceolata (Temminck) — Lanceolated Warbler
Locustella naevia (Boddaert) — Grasshopper Warbler
Locustella fluviatilis (Wolf) — River Warbler
Locustella luscinioides (Savi) — Savi's Warbler
Locustella fasciolata (G. R. Gray) — Gray's Grasshopper Warbler
Acrocephalus melanopogon (Temminck) — Moustached Warbler
Acrocephalus paludicola (Vieillot) — Aquatic Warbler
Acrocephalus schoenobaenus (Linnaeus) — Sedge Warbler
Acrocephalus agricola (Jerdon) — Paddyfield Warbler
Acrocephalus dumetorum Blyth — Blyth's Reed Warbler
Acrocephalus palustris (Bechstein) — Marsh Warbler
Acrocephalus scirpaceus (Hermann) — Reed Warbler
Acrocephalus arundinaceus (Linnaeus) — Great Reed Warbler
Acrocephalus aedon (Pallas) — Thick-billed Warbler
Hippolais pallida (Hemprich & Ehrenberg) — Olivaceous Warbler
Hippolais caligata (M. H. C. Lichtenstein) — Booted Warbler
Hippolais languida (Hemprich & Ehrenberg) — Upcher's Warbler
Hippolais olivetorum (Strickland) — Olive-tree Warbler
Hippolais icterina (Vieillot) — Icterine Warbler
Hippolais polyglotta (Vieillot) — Melodious Warbler
Sylvia sarda Temminck — Marmora's Warbler
Sylvia undata (Boddaert) — Dartford Warbler
Sylvia conspicillata Temminck — Spectacled Warbler

Sylvia cantillans (Pallas)	Subalpine Warbler
Sylvia mystacea Ménétries	Ménétries' Warbler
Sylvia melanocephala (J. F. Gmelin)	Sardinian Warbler
Sylvia melanothorax Tristram	Cyprus Warbler
Sylvia rueppelli Temminck	Rüppell's Warbler
Sylvia nana (Hemprich & Ehrenberg)	Desert Warbler
Sylvia hortensis (J. F. Gmelin)	Orphean Warbler
Sylvia nisoria (Bechstein)	Barred Warbler
Sylvia curruca (Linnaeus)	Lesser Whitethroat
Sylvia communis Latham	Common Whitethroat
Sylvia borin (Boddaert)	Garden Warbler
Sylvia atricapilla (Linnaeus)	Blackcap
Phylloscopus nitidus Blyth	Green Warbler
Phylloscopus trochiloides (Sundevall)	Greenish Warbler
Phylloscopus borealis (Blasius)	Arctic Warbler
Phylloscopus proregulus (Pallas)	Pallas' Leaf Warbler
Phylloscopus inornatus (Blyth)	Yellow-browed Warbler
Phylloscopus schwarzi (Radde)	Radde's Warbler
Phylloscopus fuscatus (Blyth)	Dusky Warbler
Phylloscopus bonelli (Vieillot)	Bonelli's Warbler
Phylloscopus sibilatrix (Bechstein)	Wood Warbler
Phylloscopus collybita (Vieillot)	Chiffchaff
Phylloscopus trochilus (Linnaeus)	Willow Warbler
Regulus regulus (Linnaeus)	Goldcrest
Regulus ignicapillus (Temminck)	Firecrest

DESCRIPTIONS

Cetti's Warbler

PLATE I

Cettia cetti (Temminck)

FH. Bouscade de Cetti   DU. Cetti's zanger
IT. Usignolo di Fiume   GR. Seidensänger   SW. Cettisångare
SP. Ruiseñor bastardo

Breeding
Present through-
out the year
Occurs in
winter

DISTRIBUTION
AND HABITAT

Iberian peninsula, central France, Italy, Greece, Romania east to E. Tian Shan Mts., and N. Afghanistan. Also
N. Africa from Morocco to Tunisia. Generally sedentary with some movement to south of range in eastern
populations. During last 35 years, a marked extension
of range has taken place to the northwest to include N.
France and S. England.

Found in low tangled vegetation, usually near water.
Also ditches, swamps, reed beds with coarse undergrowth, and thickets. Dense bushes with creepers and
brambles. Also tamarisks.

DESCRIPTION

Length 5½ in (14 cm)

Cetti's is the only European member of a subgenus
that is characterized by long soft plumage and a very
rounded tail with only 10 feathers instead of the usual

warbler's 12. Upperparts are a rich chestnut, becoming paler rufous on the rump and upper tail coverts. Supercilium is straight and dirty-white and cheeks and sides of neck are pale grey-brown. Throat is white, turning greyish at sides. Remainder of underparts dirty-white suffused with grey-brown at sides of breast and darker brown on flanks. Dark brown undertail coverts with whitish fringes reaching halfway along tail. Wings and tail blackish brown.

Juveniles are less dark on upperparts and greyer beneath.

Bill is dark purplish horn, pink at base of lower mandible.

Legs very variable from dark amber to pale pink.

Mouth also variable, reported pink, pale yellow, and orange.

Iris dark brown.

IN THE FIELD

A skulker normally identified by extraordinary song. Visually a robust, rufous bird with a pale supercilium and a ragged looking tail. Wings are short and rounded. Pronounced contrast between pale feathers on undertail coverts and dark tail feathers.

Flight between thickets and reedbeds is low and rapid. When seen perched, it appears more upright than other small, reedbed birds. Often creeps about low down in bushes or on the ground. Tail is continually flicked downwards, not upwards like most other tail-flickers.

SONG

Call note is a startling 'chik-chik' or a soft 'weet' and a harsh 'churr' of alarm. Sings usually from within dense cover, an explosive brief outburst of loud notes, ending as abruptly as it starts. The song has been transcribed as 'chee-chee-weechoo-weechoo' with many variations.

SIMILAR SPECIES

Similar in colouring to a Nightingale (*Luscinia megarhynchos*) but Cetti's is much smaller with tail less rufous than upperparts.

Unique song will distinguish Cetti's from any other bird, but in general it is chubbier and more rufous than other reed dwellers. In flight it may be taken for a Dunnock (*Prunella modularis*) at first sight, but ragged rounded tail and rufous coloration will quickly be diagnostic.

Fan-tailed Warbler

PLATE 2

Cisticola juncidis (Rafinesque)

FR. Cisticole des joncs   DU. Waaierstaartrietzanger
IT. Beccamoschino   GR. Cistensänger
SW. Grässångare   SP. Buitron

Breeding
Present through-
out the year

DISTRIBUTION AND HABITAT

Africa (except in equatorial forest), southern Europe and Mediterranean area, S. Arabia, southern Asia to China and Japan, India, Malaysia, and northern Australia.

Sedentary in Mediterranean area, but may undertake irregular winter movements. Recent spread up western coast of France almost to English Channel, but still only accidental in Britain.

Wide variety of habitat. All types of grassland, cultivated areas, road verges, as well as freshwater margins, marshes, sedge, and reeds.

DESCRIPTION

Length 4 in (10 cm)

Upperparts rufous brown with head and back streaked dark brown. No supercilium. Rufous rump.

Throat and underparts unstreaked whitish, tinged rufous buff on breast and flanks. Short rounded wings and tail. Underside of all tail feathers is strongly bordered with white and each feather has a black subterminal patch.

Immature is a rusty edition of the adult above, and pale yellowish below.

Bill dark brown above, pale horn below. Legs pale orange.

IN THE FIELD

Tiny, short-tailed bird, streaky above and whitish below. Most easily seen in breeding season display flight, a jerky undulating circle whilst uttering a weak 'dzip-dzip-dzip'. Suggests a small bright Sedge Warbler, but lack of eye stripe distinguishes it as much as size difference. Stubby, rounded wings and black and white marked tail are very noticeable. Wren-like profile in flight. Other than display flight is secretive and skulking, spending most of its time on the ground, and very difficult to see. Tail frequently cocked and spread. Notice beady eye and longish bill.

SONG

A short 'tew' call. Song is a sharp, high, rasping, repetitive note as in display flight described above. This may be performed even in the middle of the midsummer day when few other birds sing.

SIMILAR SPECIES

Unique member of large *Cisticola* genus of grass warblers to breed in or even visit Europe. They are exceptionally difficult to identify one from another, but they are sufficiently different from other genera for there to be little chance of confusion in Europe. Sedge Warbler is the nearest European species in general coloration, but apart from the Fan-tailed Warbler's size and lack of supercilium, the flight, movement, and behaviour should not cause confusion for very long.

Graceful Warbler

PLATE 2

Prinia gracilis (Lichtenstein)

FH. Prinia gracile   IT. Prinia gracile   GR. Streifenprinia

Breeding
Present through-
out the year

DISTRIBUTION AND HABITAT	Breeds in E. Egypt, Israel, Lebanon, and S. Turkey eastwards to Afghanistan and N. India. Also in E. Africa. Sedentary.

Desert scrub and dry, grassy areas. Cultivated land, tamarisks, gardens. Sometimes along river and canal banks in scrub and rank herbage. Also in sandy semi-desert country with coarse, grass tussocks or any sparse vegetation.

DESCRIPTION

Length 4 in (10 cm)

Upperparts greyish-brown strongly streaked with dark brown on head and back. Underparts whitish, tinged with grey on flanks. Outer tail feathers edged white with black subterminal patch. Flight feathers warm brown. Tail is very long (more than half total length of the bird) and graduated. There may be faint barring on the upper side of tail. Sexes alike. Juvenile is like adult but streaks on upperparts are broader and less distinct. Sides of neck and upper breast have a faint yellow tint.

Bill is black in summer, brown above and yellow below in winter. Legs are pale flesh, iris yellowish-brown, and mouth black in summer, flesh coloured in winter.

IN THE FIELD Unmistakeable, very active and perky, constantly flaunting it's long tail, flicking and opening it and occasionally twitching it from side to side. When perched frequently carries tail cocked straight up, and in flight lets it droop behind as though too heavy to be carried level.

Strong contrast between streaked upperparts and uniform pale underparts. Black subterminal patches on tail are very noticeable during tail movements. Normally in pairs or small parties keeping close to the ground or on it, where it hops about after insects. Display flight contains a fast, upward, jerky movement for a few feet, then a quick flight round before diving down to original perch or nearby. Snaps its wings with a triple noise whilst this is going on. Flight otherwise is jerky and undulating.

SONG Call is a hoarse, drawn-out 'tzeep' or a harsh alarm note of 'brrip-brrip-brrip' with variations. Song is a high-pitched wheezy warble of monotonously and persistently repeated 'zerwitze-witze-witze'.

SIMILAR SPECIES Almost none. Scrub Warbler has a shorter tail, is less rufous and has a strong head pattern. Dartford and Marmora's Warblers, hardly likely to be found in the same region as Graceful, are also obviously long tailed, but are much darker and lack the whitish underparts.

Scrub Warbler

Scotocerca inquieta (Cretzschmar)

FH. Dromoïque du desert   GR. Streifenbuschsänger

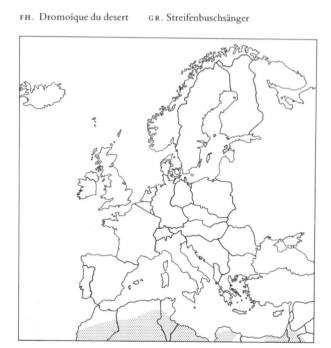

Breeding
Present through-
out the year

DISTRIBUTION AND HABITAT

South Israel and Jordan, east across Arabia to Persian Gulf, C. and E. Iran, Afghanistan to Turkestan, and N. W. India. Also in N. Africa. Sedentary.

Desert scrub, ravines, and rocky hillsides with euphorbia, cactus, and other semidesert vegetation. Sand dunes and dried-up valley floors with minimal vegetation.

DESCRIPTION

Length 4 in (10 cm)

Sexes similar. Above clear uniform sandy-brown, tinged reddish and strongly streaked on the crown. Whitish below with delicate streaks on throat and upper breast. Long, dark, strongly-rounded tail, with outermost tail feathers tipped white. Strong head pattern with clear white supercilium lined above with a black streak and below with a dark line through the eye.

Juvenile has wings and tail darker brown than adult, but with dark markings on upperparts less sharply defined.

Bill yellowish with upper mandible noticeably curved. Iris hazel. Legs yellowish-brown.

IN THE FIELD

Generally skulking, but occasionally may be observed for long periods in the open. Often in pairs or small parties. Long tail is often held erect and jerked from side to side. When alarmed will run rather than fly, but flight is usually short and straight. May be seen racing about like a mouse, it's wings and tail constantly flicking while it feeds on the ground under bushes and coarse grass.

SONG

A variety of notes of three main types. A cheerful, musical song; a loud melodious trill of about five notes descending in tone; and the alarm notes a loud but dull 'pit-pit'. Is also said to squeak like a mouse on occasion, possibly a high-pitched version of the alarm note.

SIMILAR
SPECIES

Almost none except Graceful Warbler. This has an even longer tail, but lacks strong head markings. Scrub Warbler lacks black subterminal tail spots of Graceful Warbler.

Pallas' Grasshopper Warbler

Locustella certhiola (Pallas)   PLATE 4

FH. Locustelle de Pallas   DU. Siberische snor
IT. Locustella del Pallas   GR. Streifenschwirl
SW. Starrsångare   SP. Buscarla de Pallas

DISTRIBUTION AND HABITAT

Central Asia and Siberia, north to 64°N from River Irtysh east to Manchuria, Korea, and islands north-west of Hokkaido. Migrates to India, Malaysia, Indonesia, and Philippine Is. Accidental to W. Europe.

Bushes and undergrowth along rivers and lake edges, marshes, swamps, wet meadows, or any area of damp, rank grass. In winter in rice fields.

DESCRIPTION

Length 5¼ in (13.5 cm)

Plumage is generally similar to Sedge Warbler, but has noticeably rufous rump and upper tail-coverts, the latter with blackish streaks. These contrast with grey-brown tail which is indistinctly barred. Supercilium is faint and slightly yellowish. Tail is well rounded and has blackish feather centres which broaden into a dark terminal band, especially noticeable from above. All tail feathers except central ones, have narrow greyish-white tips. Underparts are greyish-white and undertail coverts are tawny buff. Juveniles often have yellowish breasts and flanks with indistinct spots forming a broad pectoral band, and a less prominent supercilium.

Bill is blackish brown, base of lower mandible flesh-pink. Legs brownish flesh-pink at the back. Iris brown.

IN THE FIELD

Keeps well hidden. When seen appears to be a medium sized, streaky warbler with rufous upper tail contrasting with colour of lower tail, back, and particularly head. When flushed will flutter weakly for a few yards then drop out of sight again. Look for back contrasts, dark terminal band to tail, and greyish-white tips to tail feathers.

SONG

Call note is a harsh 'churr-churr'. The song opens with two separate notes, followed by a fast, repetitive string of harsh notes of varying pitch and ending with a trio of musical notes. Song is acrocephaline in character with each phrase lasting 4 or 5 seconds. Sings in flight as well as when perched.

Sedge Warbler is generally similar in colour, but Pallas'
is darker above and contrast between back and tail is
distinctive. Sedge Warbler has squarer tail, a much
more prominent supercilium, and a paler, more ginger
rump. Grasshopper Warbler behaves in similar fashion,
but Pallas' is generally browner, and rufous rump and
dark tail-end distinguish it.

Lanceolated Warbler does not have rufous rump or
pale tips to tail feathers, though upperparts are very
similar. Pallas' song is quite different to any of these and
the call note of Lanceolated is noticeably louder, albeit
similar.

Lanceolated Warbler

PLATE 5

Locustella lanceolata (Temminck)

FH. Locustelle lancéolée   DU. Temmincks rietzanger
IT. Locustella lanceolata   GR. Strichelschwirl
SW. Träsksångare   SP. Buscarla lanceolada

Breeding
Present in
summer only

DISTRIBUTION
AND HABITAT

Eastern Russia, east across Siberia to Kamchatka and south Altai Mts., across Transbaikalia to River Amur and River Ussuri. Also in Sakhalin, Japan, Korea, and Kurile Is. Migrates to India, Indochina, and Greater Sunda Is. Accidental in Western Europe.

Favours thick undergrowth and rank vegetation by reedbeds. Willows and tangled bushes or river or lake edges or by wet ditches.

DESCRIPTION

Length 4½ in (11.5 cm)

Upperparts yellowish brown with very heavy, brownish black streaking. Tail and uppertail coverts dark brown, often unstreaked. Faint buffish white supercilium. Underparts vary in background colour from white to buffy-yellow and are usually quite heavily spotted, often confined into a narrow pectoral band.

Breast spots have been described as vertical streaking below whitish throat and chin. Occasionally streaked on flanks and throat also, and undertail coverts are rufous brown with dark brown streaks. Tail is markedly rounded, short and dark-tipped.

Juveniles are tawnier brown above and yellower below. Bill is blackish brown above and pale-flesh below. Legs pinkish-brown. Iris pale to mid-brown.

IN THE FIELD   Very secretive bird which can run rapidly along the ground or through dense vegetation, which it prefers to flying away when alarmed. Visually like a small grey Grasshopper Warbler with a distinctly yellow tinge and is very heavily spotted and streaked. Has a habit of giving a fast convulsive flick of wings and tail together.

SONG   The call note is a 'chirr-chirr' harshly and aggressively uttered—louder than Pallas' Grasshopper Warbler. The song is a vibrating trill with a ventriloquist quality and recalls the stridulation of a locust. Song is normally heard only in the breeding season and only by day. Occasionally may give false starts to the song.

SIMILAR   Both song and habits are similar to the Grasshopper
SPECIES   Warbler, but Lanceolated is smaller, yellower, or greyer and more heavily streaked below. Pallas' Grasshopper Warbler is slightly larger and has a rufous rump, but the calls are extremely similar, and care must be taken to separate the birds unless the full song is heard. River Warbler usually gives only a single call note and has an unstreaked back.

Grasshopper Warbler

PLATE 6

Locustella naevia (Boddaert)

FH. Locustelle tachetée   DU. Sprinkhaanrietzanger
IT. Forapaglie macchiettato   GR. Feldschwirl
SW. Gräshoppsångare   SP. Buscarla pintoja

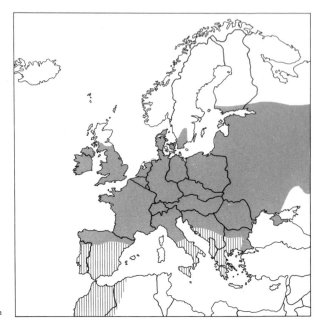

Breeding
Present in
summer only
Occurs regularly
on spring and
autumn migration

DISTRIBUTION AND HABITAT

From British Isles, France, and N. Spain eastwards across Europe and Asia to N.W. Mongolia. Migrates to southern Europe, north Africa, E. Iran, and N.W. India. Gradually extending breeding range to north and west. Undergrowth in marshes, water meadows, dry heath, hedgerows, open grassland. Often dry as well as marshy localities and may occur in crops, heather, or anywhere with sufficient growth of bushes and scrub.

DESCRIPTION

Length 5 in (13 cm)

Upperparts warm olive-brown with broad black streaks. Very faint, short, pale supercilium. Underparts may be whitish in some or pale rufous to yellowish in others. This is dimorphism, unrelated to age, sex, or area. Generally some light streaking on the breast with flanks and sides of breast buffy. Rump tinged rufous and faintly streaked, undertail coverts buff with dark streaks, contrasting with dark tail feathers. Well-rounded, longish tail which may be faintly barred. Birds with yellowish underparts have more distinct supercilia.

Adults moult after arrival in winter quarters, so that birds seen in fresh plumage in breeding area in autumn or on migration are first-year birds.

Bill is dark-brown, with lower mandible pale yellow-brown. Legs pinkish or yellowish-pink. Mouth pale pink. Iris brown.

[*Note:* Subspecies from W. Russia and Asia, *L. n. straminea,* is smaller and paler olive above, appearing much greyer in breeding season, making black streaks stand out very clearly. The mouth is yellow, not pink.]

IN THE FIELD   Very skulking and normally identified by peculiar song. Will creep and run about in undergrowth with great agility, and will prefer escape in this way rather than fly, when flushed. Best visual field marks are strongly streaked chequered back and faint eyestripe. Shape is variable, particularly in reeds where it can look short and dumpy or long and slim. A close view may reveal the very long central toe which can grasp and hold together two or more reed stems.

SONG   Call is a short 'twhit' or 'pitt' merging into a chatter when alarmed. The song is heard mostly at dusk or dawn from a low perch, a high-pitched, fast, reeling trill, lasting sometimes two minutes, a sound reminiscent of a far away electric drill. The trill appears to vary in volume, due to head-turning by the bird. Occasionally the trill will break off suddenly, only to start again almost immediately. Whilst singing the tail will vibrate.

SIMILAR SPECIES   The upperparts are less heavily streaked than Lanceolated or Pallas' Grasshopper Warbler. The general colour is less yellow than Lanceolated and the rump of Pallas' Grasshopper is more strongly rufous. In addition, Grasshopper lacks whitish-grey tips to tail feathers of Pallas' Grasshopper Warbler. In song, Savi's is somewhat similar, but is generally shorter, of a higher frequency and deeper in tone. River Warbler's song is less monotonous and is broken into short sections. River Warbler's upperparts are unstreaked and much less yellow in general tone.

River Warbler

PLATE 7

Locustella fluviatilis (Wolf)

FH. Locustelle fluviatile   DU. Krekeizanger
IT. Locustella fluviatile   GR. Schlagschwirl
SW. Flodsångare   SP. Buscarla fluvial

Breeding
Present in
summer only

Occurs regularly
on spring and
autumn migration

DISTRIBUTION AND HABITAT

From Baltic countries and southern Finland across Russia to Ural Mts. at about 60°N. East Germany, Hungary, N. Yugoslavia to Ukraine and Crimea. Migrates to E. Africa from S. Kenya south to Transvaal. Range slowly expanding to the northwest to S. Scandinavia and Holland. Otherwise accidental over extreme western Europe.

Frequents wet, wooded areas rather than marshland. Favours beech and alder or alternatively forests and parkland with plenty of undergrowth, but will usually breed by water. On migration often found in cornfields and dry, open country.

DESCRIPTION

Length 5 in (13 cm)

Upperparts uniform unstreaked, dark earth-brown. Warmer brown and very rounded tail with slightly rufous uppertail coverts. Whitish below with faint mottling on throat and breast. Flanks olive-brown and undertail coverts buffish-brown broadly tipped with white. Narrow and indistinct cream supercilium. This is a variable species, occasionally being more olive-brown above and in some the throat may be noticeably suffused with yellow. Juveniles are more rufous-brown on upperparts, and buffish-white, slightly yellow below with only the faintest breast streaks.

Bill is horn colour with pale flesh lower mandible, darker near tip. Legs flesh-pink. Mouth pale yellow. Iris hazel to dark-brown.

IN THE FIELD

Distinguished by dark brown unstreaked upperparts, but very shy and secretive, staying hidden in dense vegetation and usually located only by song. Flight is most reluctant, but it has the habit of singing from exposed bush tops within shade of trees. Look for the very rounded tail, buff and white undertail coverts, and long primaries. Streaks on breast are difficult to see from any distance.

SONG

Low harsh call note, a typical *Locustella* 'croak'. Song is a trill, somewhat like Grasshopper Warbler's, but notes are softer and slower with a rhythmic 'chuffing' like a distant steam engine. The song ends with four or five quiet 'zwee' notes. The notes of the trill are all clearly separate notes, making it more broken and less monotonous than either Savi's or Grasshopper Warblers. Sings most loudly at dawn and dusk and may sing at night.

SIMILAR SPECIES

Song should be diagnostic amongst other *Locustella* warblers. Visually, unstreaked upper parts distinguish it from Grasshopper Warbler, and conversely, mottled breast distinguishes River Warbler from both Grasshopper and Savi's Warblers. River Warbler's tail is shorter than Grasshopper's and general earth-brown upperparts are less rufous than Savi's back. Both Reed and Marsh Warblers are more rufous and paler.

Lanceolated and Pallas' Grasshopper Warblers have streaked upperparts.

Savi's Warbler

PLATE 8

Locustella luscinioides (Savi)

FH. Locustelle luscinioides   DU. Snor   IT. Salciaiola
GR. Rohrschwirl   SW. Vasssångare   SP. Buscarla unicolor

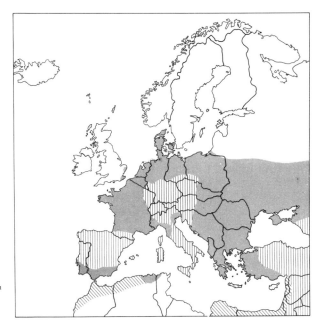

Breeding
Present in
summer only
Occurs regularly
on spring and
autumn migration
Occurs in
winter

DISTRIBUTION AND HABITAT

Iberian peninsula, S. and W. France, Netherlands, Germany, Poland, and eastwards sporadically to River Ob and Tian Shan Mts. Also N. Morocco, N. Algeria, and Crete. In recent years has begun to recolonize S. and E. England. Migrates to S. Spain, N. Africa, Nile valley, and Israel.

Marshland species inhabiting reedbeds, sedges, and low undergrowth and bushes. Swamps, fens, and areas of reed mace.

DESCRIPTION

Length $5\frac{1}{2}$ in (14 cm)

Upperparts uniformly unstreaked dark rufous-brown with head slightly darker, and rump slightly lighter, than the mantle. Short, inconspicuous, pale rufous supercilium, grey-brown earcoverts and clear, white chin. Underparts unstreaked whitish with sides of breast and flanks shaded to rich brown. Long undertail coverts pale brown with buffy tips. Tail long, wide and strongly graduated, often faintly barred. Short rounded wings. Bill usually dark brown above, paler below and dull yellow along cutting edges. Legs bright olive-brown to pale flesh colour. Mouth generally yellow. Iris dark brown. Bill, legs and mouth colour are apparently very variable as reports conflict widely.

IN THE FIELD

Sharp contrast between dark rufous back and whitish underparts and very white chin. No streaks or spots anywhere. Short rounded wings and long wide rounded tail are very noticeable. Also long undertail coverts, leaving underside of tail feathers like a dark brown band at the end of the tail. Not a shy bird, singing regularly from reed tops. Tends to cock tail and may open it. Swift, low flight over reed tops.

SONG

The only unstreaked warbler with a buzzing song. This is a reeling trill, somewhat similar to Grasshopper Warbler's, but is deeper, slower, and less prolonged. It is preceded by a series of fast 'tick-tick' notes, similar to the alarm note. These accelerate in tempo and merge into the trill. Calls consist of a thin 'tzwik' or 'szpit' which may recall a Great Tit (*Parus major*), a liquid, musical 'proo-it', and a harsh chatter. Often sings in full view, but always close to water.

SIMILAR SPECIES

Savi's superficially resembles large Reed Warbler, but song immediately distinguishes it. Visually Savi's is less rufous with a whiter breast and long undertail coverts are distinctive. Savi's wings are shorter and more rounded and tail longer and wider.

Lack of streaking will readily distinguish Savi's from Grasshopper and River Warblers and Savi's is slightly larger and less skulking than either of these.

Cetti's Warbler is much more chestnut-rufous in general appearance and has a ragged looking tail.

Marsh Warbler is noticeably smaller, paler, and greyer olive on the back. No *Acrocephalus* or *Locustella* warbler has undertail coverts as long as Savi's.

Gray's Grasshopper Warbler

Locustella fasciolata (Gray)   PLATE 3

DISTRIBUTION AND HABITAT

Central and eastern Siberia from River Ob basin east to Sakhalin, Hokkaido, Korea, Kurile Is. Migrates through E. China and Riukiu Is. to Philippine Is. and islands of S.E. Asia and Indonesia. Accidental to W. Europe. Found in bushy areas of tall, dense grass, alder and willow thickets beside riverbanks and often on damp, marshy ground with rank grass.

DESCRIPTION

Length 7 in (18 cm)

Olive-brown above with grey earcoverts, a whitish supercilium and a yellow eye ring. Unstreaked both above and below. Adults have white throat, greyish breast, and buff belly. Flanks and sides of breast are olive-buff. Margins of wing coverts and flight feathers are buff. From below, front of neck and upperbreast appear scaly and the undertail coverts are uniform rusty-yellow or orange-brown. First-year birds are warmer rufous-brown above and have underparts suffused with yellow. Supercilium is much reduced. Bill is blackish above and lower mandible chrome yellow at base, to brown at tip. Legs pale brown. Iris rich brown. Tail long and well-rounded.

IN THE FIELD

Relatively large, dark brown and whitish bird. Very shy, keeping within depths of bushes and grasses, or may run along the ground to get inside a bush. Then it may climb up inside and may be briefly visible. Will sing on the ground as well as from bush tops. Best field marks are white throat contrasting with grey breast and yellowish undertail coverts. Also large strong bill and long, pointed, graduated tail.

SONG

Loud and strong, audible at some distance, but brief. Reported as one syllable repeated five times, then two notes drawn out and finally three, rapid and descending. Entirely different from the reeling of many other *Locustella* warblers. Call is a clear, resounding 'tuti-ruti'.

SIMILAR
SPECIES

Colouring is similar to that of Savi's Warbler, but Gray's is closer to size of Great Reed Warbler. This size distinguishes it from almost every other warbler. Great Reed is more rufous above and paler below, with fainter supercilium and paler eye, although Gray's has yellow eye ring which is clear at close range. Song is similar to Pallas' Grasshopper Warbler's, but is more musical and less chattering. Thick-billed Warbler is slightly larger and looks more ungainly with its long graduated tail, but it also has a pale eye ring and may well be found in the same habitat. Thick-billed has no superciliary stripe.

Acrocephalus Warblers

Within our area these can be immediately divided into three groups: the larger birds, Great Reed, Clamorous, and Thick-billed; the streaked birds, Sedge, Moustached, and Aquatic; and the unstreaked birds, Reed, Marsh, Paddyfield, and Blyth's Reed Warblers. The first group largely divide themselves geographically and, although similar, two at least have certain features which enable identification to be made reasonably easily. Birds in the second group are also sufficiently different from each other to be fairly quickly and certainly identified, but it is in the third group where the greatest problems of identification are to be found. Whereas Reed and Marsh Warblers are reasonably common birds in our area and may be studied freely, and the subtle differences compared on frequent occasions, the other two, Blyth's Reed and Paddyfield are much rarer in the western Palaearctic and opportunities for comparison are very limited. Recent reports tend to conflict with some of the traditionally stated differences between these birds, and it is relevant to refer closely to an excellent article by D. I. M. Wallace concerning this group.

Within this third group, plumage differences are so minimal that it is impossible to describe them to the perception of individual observers. However, in March and April there runs a cline in the colour of the upperparts from bright rufous in Paddyfield, through dull rufous brown in Reed, olive-brown in Marsh to greyish-brown in Blyth's Reed. In juveniles the same cline exists, but in very much subdued colours and these appear to be much closer together than in adults. From a plumage point of view therefore, where Reed and Marsh occur together, there can be considerable difficulty in visual recognition, but where Paddyfield and Blyth's Reed occur together without Reed or Marsh, the differences are much more marked, Paddyfield looking sharp and bright in any light, whilst Blyth's Reed appears cold and olive-grey, particularly in strong light. The underparts of these two differ from yellowy-buff in Paddyfield to pale dirty white in Blyth's Reed, and there is a considerable difference in supercilia, Paddyfield having by far the most prominent of the four birds, and Blyth's Reed the shortest and least prominent.

In structure the average wing length measurements also place the four birds in order, but in a different order than that described previously. Here the two longest migrants have the first places. Marsh longest, then Reed, then Blyth's Reed, and last Paddyfield. Wings become more rounded as length decreases. Tails are roughly the same size, except for Paddyfield which is noticeably longer than the others, giving the bird a quite different shape. The bill lengths of Marsh and Reed are very nearly equal, but Blyth's Reed's is clearly longer and gives the bird 'a *Hippolais*-like head shape. Paddyfield's bill is shorter than either Marsh or Reed's. An additional aid to identification is that Blyth's Reed and Paddyfield exaggerate their tail lengths by flicking their tails.

The foregoing clearly indicates that, despite the opportunities to study them, very real difficulties exist in the separation of Reed and Marsh Warblers.

Problems of identification are made more difficult in that Cetti's Warbler is a rufous, unstreaked bird found in similar habitat and though fairly easy to distinguish it adds one more possibility to be examined or discounted after a quick first sighting. Similarly, one may add Savi's Warbler to this group, and most of the other *Locustella* warblers to the preceding, 'streaked' group, though again they should be reasonably quickly diagnosed as *Locustella* rather than *Acrocephalus*.

[See under individual species description for additional points of similarity and difference.]

Moustached Warbler

PLATE 9

Acrocephalus melanopogon (Temminck)

FH. Lusciniole à moustaches   DU. Zwartkoprietzanger
IT. Forapaglie castagnolo   GR. Tamariskensänger
SW. Tamarisksångare   SP. Carricerin real

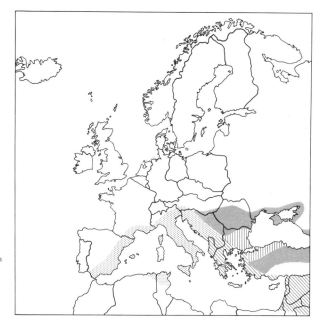

Breeding
Present in
summer only

Occurs regularly
on spring and
autumn migration

Breeding
Present through-
out the year

Occurs in
winter

DISTRIBUTION
AND HABITAT

Mediterranean Europe from S.E. Spain to Austria, Hungary, and Romania. Winters in Mediterranean basin, Israel, and Lake Chad area. A second race (*A. a. mimica*) occurs from the River Nile delta and Syria eastwards to Turkestan and Afghanistan, wintering in Iraq, Iran and into N.W. India. Accidentally to Britain.

Marshy localities, coastal thickets, ditches, reedbeds beside streams or lakes. Normally keeps to lower part of reed vegetation.

DESCRIPTION

Length 5 in (13 cm)

Back is reddish-brown streaked with black, but nape and rump are unstreaked. Prominent and distinctive white supercilium, increasing in breadth behind the eye and extending to the back of the crown where it ends

25

squarely. Cheeks and throat are also white and these white parts contrast strongly with black crown and very dark lores. Nape and necksides are rufous. Underparts whitish, buffish on flanks and undertail coverts.

First-winter birds resemble adults, except that their looser feathers make them look somewhat larger.

Bill is dark brown with base of lower mandible flesh coloured. Legs slaty blue, mouth orange-yellow, and iris bright brown.

IN THE FIELD
Looks like a very smart Sedge Warbler. Contrasts of black and white in head pattern and black and rufous on crown, nape, and back are best field marks. Habitually cocks up and spreads graduated tail. Normally skulks well down in reed cover, but may be forced by floods up into less dense parts which increases chance of observation.

SONG
Call note is a scolding 'churr', low but penetrating. Also a harder 'tshuck' which runs into a rattle of alarm, Song is less jarring and rattling than Sedge Warbler's. It is generally introduced by four high-pitched Nightingale-like notes, and then follows a fast jumble, not unmusical, with short phrases repeated four to six times. Song is usually given from a perch in reeds and with the tail depressed.

SIMILAR SPECIES
Locustella Warblers likely to be encountered in same region are smaller and darker, but may be confusing at first glance.

Aquatic Warbler is generally yellower and head is streaked, not a black crown. Aquatic does not normally cock and spread its tail.

Sedge Warbler will certainly cause most confusion and Williamson (1960) has set out concisely the main points of difference, from which review the following is taken.

Mantle	Moustached—reddish-brown
	Sedge —olive-brown
Rump	Moustached—same colour as mantle but unstreaked. This makes it appear brighter)
	Sedge —rufous, contrasting with mantle

Crown	Moustached—complete black
	Sedge —well-defined black streaks
Supercilium	Moustached—broader behind eye, white, ends square on nape
	Sedge —yellowish, uniform breadth fades into hind crown
Ear coverts	Moustached—dark brown
	Sedge —yellowish-brown
Flanks	Moustached—rusty brown
	Sedge —yellowish-brown

Eastern race is more olive on mantle and even more like a Sedge Warbler, but contrasting black and white of head pattern is still distinctive.

Aquatic Warbler

PLATE 10

Acrocephalus paludicola (Vieillot)

FH. Phragmite aquatique   DU. Waterrietzanger
IT. Pagliarolo   GR. Seggenrohrsänger
SW. Vattensångare   SP. Carricerin cejudo

Breeding
Present in
summer only
Occurs regularly
on spring and
autumn migration

DISTRIBUTION AND HABITAT	From the Baltic states, Poland, Germany, Denmark, Holland to Italy, N. Yugoslavia, and Hungary east to central Russia. Migrates through the Mediterranean area, Spain, and N. Africa to (probably) tropical Africa. Also winters in Nile valley, Greece, and Turkey. Irregular visitor to France and Britain, but may actually breed in France.

Marshy areas with rank vegetation of sedges or flags. Generally avoids reed beds (except on migration) and denser growths of willows, but usually requires some nearby open water.

DESCRIPTION	Length 5 in (13 cm)

Back is sandy buff colour heavily streaked with black. Rump is rufous and less streaked. Yellowish-buff supercilium with black brow-line above and a buff coronal band, creating a very distinctive head pattern. Buff underparts with dark stripes on breast and flanks which are very conspicuous even in winter. Tail is well rounded and bright rufous in colour. Tail feathers appear pointed.

Juveniles have bright sandy buff upperparts, where adults are much greyer olive on mantle and nape. Wing coverts of juveniles are reddish buff streaked with black, and autumn adults' coverts and flight feathers are worn and faded to greyish-brown with no rufous in the wing. Adults are paler buff below than younger birds.

Bill blackish, flesh-coloured below. Legs pinkish-flesh. Iris brown.

IN THE FIELD
A distinctly yellowish bird. Buff crown stripe and long, buff supercilium are easily seen as is streaked, rusty rump and russet tail. Pointed tips to tail feathers are also a good field mark. More skulking than Sedge Warbler and may sometimes be seen feeding on the ground. Adults are very shy and cautious, but young birds may show great curiosity.

SONG
Call is a scolding 'tack'. Song is similar to Sedge Warbler, but the song phrases are shorter and more distinct, and it is not so rich and varied. The song is often given in a short song-flight. Song contains frequently repeated syllables as in 'errr-di-di-di-di' and 'orr-dyu-dyu-dyu.

SIMILAR SPECIES
Like a sandy Sedge Warbler, but more skulking. Supercilium is buff versus white in Sedge Warbler. Great care must be taken in separating young Sedge Warblers which have a buff stripe, often not noticeably fainter, down the crown centre. Head pattern should otherwise separate Aquatic from all other *Acrocephalus* Warblers. Rump in Sedge Warbler is unstreaked and in flight the sandy, streaked back and rump of Aquatic Warbler show up well.

Aquatic is much sandier than Moustached Warbler or any of the streaked *Locustella* warblers.

Sedge Warbler

PLATE 11

Acrocephalus schoenobaenus (Linnaeus)

FH. Phragmite des joncs   DU. Rietzanger   IT. Forapaglie
GR. Schilfrohrsänger   SW. Sävsångare   SP. Carricerin comun

Breeding
Present in
summer only
Occurs regularly
on spring and
autumn migration

DISTRIBUTION AND HABITAT

Europe and Asia from Scandinavia, Britain, and Iberian peninsula east to River Yenisei, Altai Mts., Turkestan, and Transcaspia. Also N. Africa from Morocco to Algeria. Migrates through Mediterranean region and Middle East to winter in tropical and southern Africa from Nigeria to Arabia and to Natal.

Willow thickets and other bushes near water, often with undergrowth of reeds or sedge. Also osiers, along ditches and hedgerows, and not infrequently on drier ground in bush locations.

DESCRIPTION

Length 5 in (13 cm)

Back olive-brown with black striations, but rump unstreaked and ginger rufous in colour. Rump contrasts well with streaked back and dark tail. Sides of head are brownish while crown is heavily streaked, the streaking

being accentuated by a conspicuous creamy supercilium. Underparts are creamy white tinged with rufous
on the flanks and sides. Tail is slightly rounded. Juvenile
birds have all the upper parts brighter and more yellowish-brown. Wing feathers are edged with buff and there
are sparse spots on throat and breast. Autumn adults are
duller and greyer especially on nape and upper mantle,
and wing and tail feathers appear very abraded. Juveniles tend to show crown streaks, strongly enough to
cause confusion with Aquatic Warblers.

Bill blackish-brown above with base of lower mandible yellowish. Legs pale-grey to yellowish-grey. Mouth
orange. Iris brown.

IN THE FIELD   Best field marks are creamy supercilium, heavily
streaked olive upperparts and unstreaked, ginger rump
contrasting with dark, squarish tail. Very active bird,
but skulks like other reed-bed warblers. Often emerges
from low vegetation to sing noisily, and may also sing
from a perch or in a short vertical display flight. Adept
at moving through dense low vegetation and may creep
about on the ground. Flight is generally low, over short
distances, with the tail noticeably spread and drooping.

SONG   Call is a scolding 'tuck' often rapidly repeated, and a
harsh 'churr'. The song is a loud, rapid sequence of
harsh, chattering notes and whistles, and sweeter musical ones, with much repetition mixed with long trills and
frequent high 'chirrups'. Harsh notes are repeated rapidly and increased in tempo into a trill. Then they
suddenly slow down to a short series of calls resembling
the alarm call, but softer. Sings both by day and night in
the breeding season, but strongest at dawn and dusk.
Whilst singing it may move jerkily up a reed stem.

SIMILAR   Easily distinguished from commonest cohabitant of
SPECIES   European reed beds, the Reed Warbler, by supercilium,
rump, and streaking.

Dark-crowned adults may be confused with
Moustached Warbler (see under that species).

Aquatic Warbler has a streaked rump and is more
yellow generally in colour. Juvenile Sedge Warblers
have crown stripes which can be very conspicuous and
this feature combined with their more yellowy-brown

plumage makes them very confusable with Aquatic Warblers. Rumps are safer diagnostic features, the un-streaked ginger of the Sedge Warbler showing up well in flight.

The song is more varied and rapid than the Reed Warbler's and more rhythmical. All other *Acrocephalus* Warblers except Aquatic and Moustached have un-streaked upperparts, and Sedge Warblers can be sepa-rated from *Locustella* Warblers, in particular Grass-hopper Warbler, by the more pronounced supercilium and less mottled back of the Sedge. The tail is squarer-ended than those of the Moustached, Aquatic, or Grass-hopper Warblers.

Paddyfield Warbler

PLATE 12

Acrocephalus agricola (Jerdon)

FH. Rousserolle isabelle   IT. Cannaiola di Jerdon
GR. Feldrohrsänger   SP. Carricero agricola

Breeding
Present in
summer only

DISTRIBUTION AND HABITAT

From S. Russia eastward across Kirghiz steppes to central Mongolia and Sinkiang. Russian Turkestan south to E. Iran and N. Afghanistan. Migrates to S. Iran and Afghanistan through Pakistan to C. India. Very rare vagrant to W. Europe.

Streams and lake edges with reeds, sedges and willows. Also any damp locality with areas of long grass or in unkempt gardens. Avoids denser and more extensive reed beds, but appears to need water nearby at all times.

DESCRIPTION

Length 5 in (12.5 cm)

Upperparts sandy-brown with bright rufous tinge. Crown darker and rump and uppertail coverts russet. White supercilium growing noticeably broader behind the eye. Wings and tail brown with rufous edges to feathers. Underparts whitish with ochre tinge on breast and flanks. Variously described as 'pale reddish-brown above' and 'sandy buff below'.

Juveniles are more olive-brown on mantle but have bright rufous upper tail feathers and the supercilium is tinged with rufous. Adults in autumn plumage markedly brighter and more russet than in spring on upperparts, and purer and brighter below.

Bill dark horn above and pale flesh below. Legs very pale brown. Mouth pale yellow. Iris olive-brown.

IN THE FIELD   Similar to Reed Warbler but more conspicuous supercilium and brighter coloration generally. Less timorous than other reed-bed Warblers, but if pursued goes quickly into cover or may fly away from water habitat if only briefly. A good field mark is the rufous edging to secondary wing feathers. Has a noticeably shorter tail than Reed Warbler and a cockier, jauntier appearance.

SONG   Call a sharp 'chik-chik'. Song similar to Marsh Warbler's but softer and without harsh whistling notes. Highly developed mimicry, in particular of surrounding birds such as tits, wagtails, and coot. Remains constantly in trees whilst singing.

SIMILAR
SPECIES   (For general comments on distinction between Paddyfield, Reed, Marsh, and Blyth's Reed see introduction to genus *Acrocephalus* on page 23.)

In summary, Paddyfield has brighter colour generally and more conspicuous supercilium than other three species. Paler and more rufous above than Reed or Blyth's Reed Warbler. Less olive generally than Marsh Warbler. Rump is rustier than any other unstreaked *Acrocephalus* Warbler.

Savi's Warbler, being unstreaked above may be confused, but Savi's is a much darker-backed and sombre coloured bird and the supercilium is not as conspicuous as Paddyfield's.

Blyth's Reed Warbler

PLATE 13

Acrocephalus dumetorum Blyth

FH. Rousserolle des buissons   DU. Blyth's kleine karekiet
IT. Cannaiola di Blyth   GR. Buschrohrsänger
SW. Busksångare   SP. Carricero de Blyth

Breeding

Present in summer only

Occurs regularly on spring and autumn migration

NOTE

A proposal has been written on the possibility of Blyth's Reed Warbler being a race of the African Reed Warbler, *Acrocephalus baeticatus*. For the purposes of comparison with other European warblers, I have here retained *Acrocephalus dumetorum* as a separate species. [See C. H. Fry, K. Williamson, and I. J. Ferguson-Lees (1974). *Ibis* **116,** 340–6.]

DISTRIBUTION
AND HABITAT

S. Finland and Baltic states south to the Ukraine and east across Siberia to River Yenisei; Kirghiz steppes, Aral–Caspian region to E. Iran; Altai Mts. to N.W. Mongolia, Turkestan, and N. Afghanistan. Migrates to Pakistan, India, Sri Lanka, and Burma.

Recent westward spread into Scandinavia, but very rare vagrant to other areas of western Europe.

35

Marshy localities with trees and bushes, also low dense vegetation, wood edges, rank grass in ditches, neglected gardens, and orchards. Frequently found near to water, but by no means always.

DESCRIPTION

Length 5 in (12.5 cm)

Greyish olive-brown above becoming greyer into late summer; after autumn body-moult becomes brighter and more greenish olive-brown with rump often slightly rufous. Indistinct buff supercilium. Whole underparts pale buff, slightly paler on chin, throat, and belly.

Iris light brown. Bill mid-brown above, flesh-coloured below. Legs dark grey. Mouth bright yellow. Tail slightly rounded.

IN THE FIELD

Solitary. In winter generally not near water, but stays in thick cover, hedgerows, tamarisk, bracken, etc. Wings are short and rounded, and bill is longer and thinner and forehead steeper than other *Acrocephali*. Very similar to several other species (see below) but appears as a small edition of Great Reed Warbler with difference in mouth colour and is less catholic in its habitat preferences. The short rounded wings make the tail appear exaggeratedly long and the flight is whirring and Wren-like.

SONG

Single harsh note 'tshuk' uttered at intervals of a few seconds. Occasionally doubled as 'Tshuk-tshuk'; also a softer 'tup-tup' or a sharp 'churr'. Song normally heard only in spring, and is similar to Marsh Warbler, rich and varied, long and loud, but at much slower tempo. Strongly imitative and frequently sings at night. Usually sings in full view and the typical 'tshuk-tshuk' may be heard frequently in the song.

SIMILAR SPECIES

See introduction to genus *Acrocephalus* for general comments. Very difficult to separate from Reed, Marsh, and Paddyfield Warblers.

Marsh Warbler is closest in coloration and song. Blyth's Reed is browner and less olive on upperparts. Also darker and less rusty on upperparts than Reed Warbler. More arboreal than either and has longer tail and longer and thinner bill than either. First-winter birds of all three species are closer together in colour and are virtually inseparable in the field.

Paddyfield is russet on upperparts, not olivaceous, and is found far more exclusively in reed beds.

Confusion may occur in separating Blyth's Reed from Booted Warbler, but Booted has tail less steeply graduated and has a distinctive white edge to outer tail feathers.

Marsh Warbler

PLATE 13

Acrocephalus palustris (Bechstein)

FH. Rousserolle verderolle   DU. Bosrietzanger
IT. Cannaiola verdognola   GR. Sumpffrohrsänger
SW. Kärrsångare   SP. Carricero poliglota

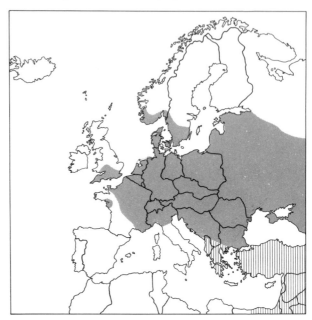

Breeding
Present in
summer only
Occurs regularly
on spring and
autumn migration

DISTRIBUTION
AND HABITAT

Southern England and parts of France across central Europe between S. Scandinavia and N. Italy and Greece in the south, eastwards to Ural Mts. Also Transcaucasia and Aral–Caspian region and N. Iran. Migrates to E. Africa and south to Natal.

Areas of dense, low vegetation near fresh water. Also thickets, ditches, stream banks, osier beds, and sometimes crops and gardens, particularly with pea and bean plants. Particularly partial to large patches of nettles.

DESCRIPTION

Length 5 in (12.5 cm)

Greenish, olive-brown above, browner on rump, but not as rufous as in Reed Warbler. Whitish below, suffused with buff, especially on flanks. Slight pale supercilium. Undertail coverts warm buff. Noticeably white throat patch.

Juveniles are tawny above, tending to a rufous tinge on rump, compared to autumn adults with very worn wings and tail, being noticeably greyer than in spring.

Bill dark brown above, pale, yellowish horn below. Legs flesh coloured with yellowish tinge. Mouth yellow or orange yellow, but not sufficiently distinct from Reed Warbler to be diagnostic, especially in young birds. Iris olive-brown.

IN THE FIELD Like other reed-bed warblers is shy and keeps to close cover. Sidles up and down reed or grass stems and stays very active either in this environment or in the bushes and low vegetation which it seems to favour. Appears to be a uniform olive-coloured bird with no distinguishing plumage marks and is exceptionally difficult to identify without close study. Beware of fluffed-out throat feathers giving greyish impression.

SONG Alarm note is a high-pitched churring or a loudly repeated 'tic', or 'tic-shizz', and it may also give a subdued chatter of 'tic'-like variations. Loud bill-snapping may be heard when alarmed. The song is very rich and diverse and has a flowing quality and fullness which immediately separates it from either Sedge or Reed Warbler's song. A long list of imitations has been claimed, but finch and starling-like sounds are particularly common and are mixed in with typically acrocephaline squawks. Occasionally the bird being imitated seems to take over completely and the harsh notes disappear. The song is usually uttered rapidly with the inclusion of many whistling notes and canary-like trills. Singing is usually confined to daytime, and when in full flow, the male will perch on an exposed twig at the top of a bush or tree, swelling out his throat, opening his mouth widely, and occasionally fanning his tail and jerking it sideways in mid-song.

SIMILAR SPECIES For general comments see under introduction to genus *Acrocephalus* (page 23). Adults in spring and summer normally separated from Reed Warbler by coloration of upperparts, especially the rump. In Marsh this is brownish-olive similar to mantle. In Reed it is rusty and contrasts with mantle. Marsh Warbler's supercilium is shorter and clearer than Reed Warbler's, and its throat is whiter. Marsh's legs are usually paler than Reed's and Marsh is less wholly aquatic than Reed. Marsh tends to look bulkier, more like a *Sylvia* warbler, and its behaviour is less skulking and more excitable than a Reed Warbler's. Songs are very different and Marsh's song is much less harsh than that of Sedge Warbler.

Reed Warbler

PLATE 14

Acrocephalus scirpaceus (Hermann)

FH. Rousserolle effarvatte   DU. Kleine karekiet   IT. Cannaiola
GR. Teichrohrsänger   SW. Rörsångare   SP. Carricero comun

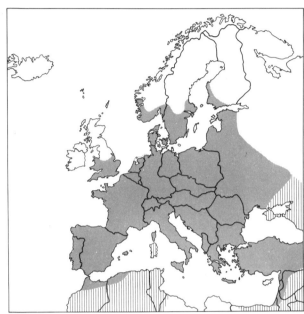

Breeding
Present in
summer only
Occurs regularly
on spring and
autumn migration

DISTRIBUTION
AND HABITAT

From Iberian peninsula to S. and E. Britain, S. Finland, and S. Russia. Also through N.W. Africa and S. Europe eastwards to S. Iran. Distribution in western Russia is discontinuous. On passage through Mediterranean area, N. Africa and S.W. Asia to E. Africa.

Reed beds, osier beds, and other rank vegetation or bushes near water. In Central Europe regularly in drier situations such as parks and gardens. In winter quarters and on migration may be found far from water in bush or cultivated country.

DESCRIPTION

Length 5 in (12.5 cm)

Upperparts warm olive-brown becoming, as summer progresses, darker on the head and more rufous on the rump. Whitish underparts turning to buff on the flanks and more definitely buff on undertail coverts. Narrow, ill-defined supercilium from nostrils over to just behind eye. Tail dark brown with very narrow, whitish tips and fringes to inner webs. Juveniles are rustier brown, especially on the rump and wing coverts. Also duskier on breast and flanks.

Bill dark brown, yellowish below. Legs medium to dark brown but varied. Mouth orange. Iris pale brown.

IN THE FIELD   Normally shy and keeps well within cover. Rarely seen outside reed beds actually over water. Clings to reed stems sidling up and down restlessly and hopping quickly from one to another. May briefly fly to a nearby willow or sedge but will return to reeds again before long. Flies only short distances, mostly over reed tops or open patches of water with tail spread and drooping. Appears to be a uniform brown bird with no distinct eyestripe and of a pronounced rufous colour without dark markings or streaks.

SONG   Usual call note is a low hard 'churr', which when alarmed is lengthened into a hoarse rattle. The 'churr' phrases form the basis of the song which is more subdued than that of Sedge Warbler. The song is a mixture of trills and short phrases repeated frequently. There are 3–4 notes to a phrase which are high, harsh, squawking sounds and these are interspersed with more musical notes, but the whole has a uniformity and seems slow. More regular in tempo than Sedge Warbler. Often mimetic, though not to the same extent as Marsh Warbler, and during breeding period, often sings at night.

SIMILAR SPECIES   Due to similarity of habitat, must first be separated from Sedge Warbler. Visually, the pronounced supercilium of the streaked Sedge Warbler should present no problems, but the songs of the two can sound similar. Much more difficult is separation between unstreaked *Acrocephalus* Warblers (see general comments in introduction to genus *Acrocephalus*, page 23). Geographically Reed and Marsh need distinguishing, being both slim, active reed birds.

Reed Warblers are warmer coloured, darker just in front of the eye, more rufous on uppertail feathers and have a dirty white eyering compared to Marsh Warbler's pure white.

Reed Warbler is usually confined to reed beds and their borders whilst a Marsh Warbler is more often seen in willows, osiers, and other low vegetation.

Reed Warbler's legs are normally grey-brown, darker than Marsh's pale flesh-coloured legs.

Reed Warblers tend to adopt a less horizontal posture than Marsh and tend to look less bulky.

Song differences are much easier to distinguish, Reed Warbler's harsh chattering mixture of 'churr-churr' and 'jag-jag-jag' notes being much less melodious and varied than Marsh Warblers.

Great Reed Warbler

PLATE 15

Acrocephalus arundinaceus (Linnaeus)

FH. Rousserolle turdoïde   DU. Grote karekeit
IT. Cannareccione   GR. Drosselrohrsänger
SW. Trastsångare   SP. Carricero tordal

Breeding
Present in
summer only
Occurs regularly
on spring and
autumn migration

DISTRIBUTION
AND HABITAT

Breeds in Europe from Iberian peninsula, France, Netherlands, Denmark, S. Sweden, and Baltic countries eastwards to central Russian Altai and south to Transcaspian region, Mesopotamia, and coast of E. Morocco and Algeria. Winters in W. and S.C. Africa. During this century, the range has expanded to the northwest to include France and Scandinavia, and it occurs in S.E. England with increasing frequency.

Prefers dense, large reed beds with some open water and with nearby small trees and bushes. Also margins of fresh water, including lakes, rivers, ponds, and canals. On passage in ditches, gardens, and dryer areas such as heath and scrub country. May be seen perching on bushes, posts or telegraph wires.

Note: The Great Reed Warbler has been treated variously as one, two, or three species. For European review *Acrocephalus arundinaceus* covers practically the whole area. The form separated as the Clamorous Reed Warbler, *Acrocephalus stentoreus* (Hemprich and Ehrenberg) is resident in Egypt and Israel. For differences between *A. arundinaceus* and *A. stentoreus* see below, but as they are very slight and subtle, I have confined description to *A. arundinaceus*.

[See E. Stresemann and J. Arnold (1949). *J. Bombay nat. Hist. Soc.* **48,** 428–43; A. Zahavi (1957). *Ibis* **99,** 600–7.]

DESCRIPTION

Length 7½ in (17–18 cm)

Similar in colouring to Reed Warbler. Adult upperparts warm olive-brown, crown darker brown. Rump and uppertail coverts more tawny. Chin, throat, and centre of belly white, remaining underparts including undertail coverts creamy to tawny buff, darker on flanks. Occasionally faint brown streaks on throat. Pale and indistinctive supercilium. Tail well rounded.

First-winter birds are generally buffier below and adults in autumn may show grey blotches on shoulders and rump. Bill heavy, dark brown above, pinkish-flesh below with brown tip. Mouth orange red. Legs pale brownish-grey and iris yellowish.

IN THE FIELD

The largest European Warbler. Overall brown colour, supercilium, and lack of any sharply defined identification points generally determine identity and this is reinforced by strident song. When the head is clearly visible, the bill is noticeably long and straight, appearing to be of a uniform depth almost throughout its length. Less secretive or skulking than Reed Warbler. Its thrush-size makes it conspicuous and it easily attracts attention when it flies with downward spread tail and fast wingbeats, jerkily and for short distances over reed tops or open water. Frequently perches in the open on bushes or even telegraph wires.

SONG

Call note is a harsh 'tack' or 'chock' and a deep gutteral croak. Alarm call is a strident chatter. The song may be delivered from inside reed cover or from high on an exposed perch, and is somewhat similar to those of

Sedge or Reed Warblers, but much louder, harsher and more croaking with a deep frog-like 'karra-karra-karra-keek' or 'gurk-gurk-gurk' interspaced with shriller and more squeaky sections. Sometimes strongly imitative. Sings by night as well as day and may continue song for many minutes with such intense concentration that it seems oblivious of approaching humans.

SIMILAR SPECIES

Once this bird is established as a warbler, there can be no mistaking it within the European area. Initially it may be separated from others, easily done if the flight is observed, but the supercilium and bill length also serve to identify it. Most easily likened to a double-sized Reed Warbler.

Amongst fringe area Warblers, Thick-billed Warbler has a longer, more graduated tail, a shorter, thicker bill and no pale supercilium.

There is danger of confusion with Clamorous Reed Warbler in extreme southeast of the area. Where they can be found together, the following points may help to distinguish one from another. Great Reed is generally darker, less grey and buffer below. It has a more obvious supercilium and a shorter darker bill than the Clamorous, and the tail appears to be shorter and less well rounded. Clamorous generally appears to be longer, slimmer, and paler than Great Reed. More helpful are the songs, the Clamorous having a thinner, reedier, higher-pitched song with more broken rhythm and less repetition.

Thick-billed Warbler
PLATE 15

Acrocephalus aedon (Pallas)

FH. Rousserolle à gros bec   IT. Cannareccione beccogrosso
GR. Dickschnabelsänger   SP. Carricero picogordo

DISTRIBUTION AND HABITAT

Southern Siberia from the River Ob and northern Mongolia eastward to Manchuria, Amurland, and N.E. China. Migrates to S.E. China, Indochina, India, Malaysia, and Andaman Is. Accidental to Europe.

Marshy places with bushes or low trees close to water, or at forest edges, in gardens, plantations, or by roadsides. Also hazel thickets and thinner birch forests. In winter in tea and coffee plantations.

DESCRIPTION

Length 8 in (19 cm)

Resembles Great Reed Warbler in general size, shape, and coloration. Upperparts olive-brown with distinctly rufous rump. Uppertail coverts fulvous. Lores white, sides of head light olive-brown. Eye ring pale, no superciliary stripe. Wings pale brown, margined with olive. Tail long and graduated, pale fulvous brown, edged with darker buff. Throat and centre of belly white, remainder of underparts brownish-buff. First-winter birds more rufous on back than adults.

Bill is very stout and noticeably shorter than Great Reed Warbler's. Dark brown above edged with yellow and yellow below. Legs pinkish tinged with blue-grey. Iris hazel and mouth bright pink.

IN THE FIELD

A shy bird, more likely to be seen in trees than reeds, though will usually ascend to open bush or treetops to sing. Occasionally raises its crown feathers into a conspicuous crest and moves its tail in a shrike-like manner. A heavy, rather ungainly bird with long tail and very rounded wings, but again resembles a shrike in its flight which is slow but very agile.

SONG

Call note is a very distinct 'chok-chok' (its vernacular name in Russia) coarsely uttered, usually from within a bush. The song is loud and resonant with snatches of mimicry and resembles somewhat an Icterine Warbler's with many Nightingale-like notes.

47

SIMILAR
SPECIES

Nearest to Great Reed Warbler, but has a longer, more graduated tail, a thicker, shorter bill, and no superciliary stripe. Generally shyer than Great Reed Warbler. May also be confused initially with a bulbul or a shrike, especially if first seen in flight, but generally coloration is quite unlike that of any shrike likely to be found within its distribution area, and the posture and actions are quite different from those of a bulbul.

Hippolais

Hippolais warblers demand an approach to specific identification which is quite different and much more exacting than in identifying other warblers. Every possible detail must be noted because plumage patterns alone are insufficient for certain diagnosis. Characteristics of habitat, behaviour, structure, and calls must be recorded as accurately as possible and rechecked at different times and from different angles if possible. A most excellent review of the field identification of *Hippolais* warblers has been written by D. I. M. Wallace (1964) and this is worth studying in close detail. Wallace recommends the following points should be kept in mind in determining the correct species of *Hippolais*.

(i) A detailed plumage description is essential, but can be insufficient on its own. Great care is needed in noting colours which can alter markedly in different lights.

(ii) Observe size, shape, and structure. Head shape is important, as well as length and shape of the wings and tail when flying and when perched,

(iii) Observe bill, legs, iris, gape—particularly for colour, but in the case of bill, relate the size to the head length and this ratio to other well-known birds.

(iv) Note actions, tail flicking, hovering, feeding habits, etc.

(v) Describe all calls and song as accurately as possible—length of phrases, repetition of note or phrase, musical or harsh notes, rise or fall in strength, speed, or tone. Compare notes or phrases with birds you know well.

The general characteristics of the members of this genus are that, apart from the Booted Warbler, they are all quite large, rather heavily built, and without the grace and delicateness of a *Phylloscopus*, or the alertness and jerkiness of a *Sylvia*. Their bodies often appear plump or pear-shaped with a belly-down appearance, and they have a noticeably flat back and tail line. Their heads are prominent and, again except for the Booted

Warbler, their bills are broad, strong, and often notice-ably long. They sometimes look short-tailed in the field as they appear to carry more bulk forward of their legs than behind. They appear clumsy and careless in their movements through foliage, and they have a most characteristic way of picking berries off a spray, using a sharp backward tug of the head.

Typically, *Hippolais* warblers possess green or grey plumage and relatively long wings and tail. Tails are nearly square-ended and all have very short under tail coverts. All the species have plumage without strong patterns, apart from short supercilia, eye rings, and pale edges to inner flight feathers, and even these characters vary in individuals and according to age and season.

The two warblers most confusable with *Hippolais* species are the Marsh Warbler and the Garden Warbler. A poor view of the latter can be very convincing as a *Hippolais*, and this possibility must be quickly ruled out by its lack of supercilium and its short, deep bill and round head compared to the streamlined set of forehead and bill typical of *Hippolais*.

Wing shape is the single most important character in determination of a *Hippolais*. The Olive Tree, Icterine, and Upcher's Warblers have the longest wings. In all three the tips of the folded primaries, when perched, either reach fully, or end beyond, the ends of the uppertail coverts; and the slim point of the folded primaries beyond the secondaries represents about one-third of the whole visible wing length. In Olivaceous, Melodious, and Booted Warblers, the tips of the folded primaries fall short of, or occasionally only just reach, the ends of the uppertail coverts; and the slim point of the folded primaries projecting beyond the secondaries, represents only a quarter, sometimes less, of the total visible wing length. In long-winged species, the bun-ched end of the primaries is about equal to the length of the secondaries. The shape of wings when flying is best observed when either just taking off or about to land, as wings are then fully extended and undistorted.

Wallace has given a field key which may be helpful in trying to identify *Hippolais* species, but is in any case a useful summary of the major points of structure and plumage.

A. LONG-WINGED

1. Bill very prominent, long and deep; body large; inner wing feathers prominently edged whitish; broad supercilium. Olive Tree Warbler.

2. Bill long; body quite large; tail dark with whitish edges; tail often cocked. Upcher's Warbler.

3. Bill fairly long; body medium; upperparts greenish-olive; inner wing feathers prominently edged yellow forming conspicuous panel. Normal adult Icterine Warbler.

4. Bill and body as 3; upperparts greyish; inner wing feathers edged whitish but forming inconspicuous wing panel. Variant adult and immature Icterine Warbler.

B. SHORT-WINGED

1. Bill prominent; length exaggerated by flat crown; body medium sized; eye ring often noticeable and whitish. Olivaceous Warbler.

2. Bill strong but length diminished by round head; body medium; upperparts greenish-brown; pale edges of inner wing feathers not forming panel; underparts yellow. Normal adult Melodious Warbler.

3. Bill, head shape, and body as 2; upperparts brownish; wings unmarked. Variant adult and immature Melodious Warbler.

4. Bill short (like *Phylloscopus* from side); round head; body small; no obvious plumage characters. Booted Warbler.

Olivaceous Warbler

PLATE 16

Hippolais pallida (Hemprich and Ehrenberg)

FH. Hypolaïs pâle   DU. Vale spotvogel   IT. Canapino pallido
GR. Blassspötter   SW. Blek gulsångare   SP. Zarcero palido

Breeding
Present in
summer only

Occurs regularly
on spring and
autumn migration

Breeding
Present through-
out the year

DISTRIBUTION
AND HABITAT

S. Iberian peninsula and N. Africa to Lake Chad, Lower Egypt, and S.E. Europe east through Turkey, Israel, Iraq, Iran to N. Afghanistan and Russian Turkestan to the Tian Shan and Tadzhikistan. Migrates to W. Africa, Upper Nile region, and S.W. Arabia.

Two distinct races occur in Europe, *H. p. opaca* in the southwest and *H. p. elaeica* in the south-east of Europe and the Near East. *H. p. opaca* inhabits gardens and orchards, prefers tall trees to bushes and is very active. It appears fearless and tame compared to *H. p. elaeica* which is shy and skulking. *H. p. elaeica* occurs in bushy areas, usually near the ground in wet valley bottoms up to about 6000 ft.

Both races have occurred in N.W. Europe, accidentally in Britain.

DESCRIPTION
Length 5¼ in (13.5 cm)

Both races have olive-green upperparts with a greyish tinge in *H. p. opaca*, and a richer green tinge in *H. p. elaeica*, but when adults get to winter quarters, the dominant colours tend to be reversed. Both races wear to greyish-olive before migrating. Wings and tail are brown with outer two pairs of tail feathers dirty white with whiter tips. This white area of the tail persists even in worn birds. There is no pale centre-wing panel at any time. Underparts are creamy or pale buff with the throat whiter. In spring, underparts may occasionally have a yellowish wash. Pale grey eye ring and short supercilium. Legs very variable from bluish-grey to grey-brown. Bill is dark-brown above and yellowish-horn below. It is very prominent and wide and the length is further exaggerated by the flat crown. Mouth orange-yellow; iris sepia-brown.

IN THE FIELD
Appears to be a plump, pale bird, very similar in size and shape to Icterine, particularly at long range, but Olivaceous seems to have more depth to its body. Characteristically heavy in flight, appearing to labour and flutter, particularly when taking off or in low-level flight. Olivaceous Warblers have a shallow tail flick and move their tails continuously whilst feeding. Lack of any green or yellow colour, coupled with flat crown, long bill and short rounded wings are the best field marks. Of all *Hippolais* warblers, the Olivaceous' plumage can alter most with different sunlight and shadow effects. White tail feathers should also be looked for.

SONG
Rather loud and harsh, recalling *Acrocephalus* warblers, but noticeably less harsh and less varied than Sedge Warbler. Song is usually given from thick cover. Call note is a clear 'tchack-tchack', similar to that of Icterine. Alarm note is a quiet ticking.

SIMILAR SPECIES
Inevitably confused with Garden Warbler, even in voice. Head shape and bill are best differences. Also Olivaceous has more prominent supercilium, though still faint; very short undertail coverts and whitish tips to tail feathers.

Compared with *Acrocephalus* warblers, Olivaceous' tail is squarer (though still rounded at corners) and undertail coverts are much shorter. Compared with other *Hippolais* warblers, lack of yellow distinguishes it from normal Icterine or Melodious. Compared with washed-out Icterine and Melodious, whitish tips to tail feathers and tail movement distinguish Olivaceous. Also Icterine's wings are much longer and more pointed than Olivaceous'. Olive Tree Warbler is a larger, much greyer bird with an even longer bill, and very long, pointed wings. Upcher's Warbler also has long wings and often cocks its tail up, but shows more and clearer white on the tail than Olivaceous. Booted Warbler is smaller than Olivaceous with a short bill and round head, but small species of *H. p. elaeica* may sometimes be confused with Booted. Booted is more brown-grey on the upperparts. The lack of conspicuous features and the variety of colour evident with changing light make this a most difficult bird to identify.

Booted Warbler

PLATE 12

Hippolais caligata (Lichtenstein)

FR. Hypolaïs russe   IT. Canapino asiatico
GR. Buschspötter   SP. Zarcero escita

Breeding
Present in
summer only

DISTRIBUTION
AND HABITAT

Northern and Central Russia east to N.W. Mongolia and W. Sinkiang and south to S. Iran. Migrates to India and S.W. Arabia. Accidental to Europe.

Found in bushes, forest edges, gardens, hedgerows, and cultivated areas. Also scrub and semidesert regions, birchwoods, and tamarisk thickets.

DESCRIPTION

Length 4½ in (11–12 cm)

In breeding plumage greyish-brown above and white below, with faint buffy wash on breast, flanks, and undertail coverts. Head slightly darker than mantle and fairly distinct but short, buffish-white supercilium and narrow eye ring. Outer tail feathers very faintly lined white, and white at the tips. Penultimate feathers also white at the tips. Wing feathers lack white edges.

55

Underparts dull white with buff or olive-grey wash on flanks and sides of chest.

First-winter birds are greyish-olive above, whereas adults in autumn have warm brownish-olive upperparts.

Bill much smaller than any other *Hippolais*, more phylloscopine in appearance, dark brown in colour with base of lower mandible pale pink. Legs pale brown, mouth bright yellow and iris olive-brown.

IN THE FIELD

Extremely shy and skulking. Appears to be a small edition of an Olivaceous Warbler, but has much smaller bill and more buff on the flanks. Smaller bill is accentuated by the rounder head. Wings are very short and rounded, apparently almost fan-shaped. Body is small and compact. Though typically a *Hippolais* body-shape, when perched it looks very like a Chiffchaff.

SONG

Strong, loud, and babbling, but musical. Consists of variations on 'chrek, chrek' call note. Other call notes are a single or double 'chick', which is a subdued version of Upcher's Warbler's loud, distinctive 'chuck'. This note with Booted Warbler is reminiscent of a *Sylvia* warbler. Alarm note is a low churring noise. Sings during breeding season by night as well as day.

SIMILAR SPECIES

Compared to Olivaceous Warbler, Booted is smaller, more buff on flanks and a rounder head. Booted is generally grey-brown above in spring on upperparts, where Olivaceous is olive-brown.

Compared with smaller *Acrocephalus* warblers, Booted has short undertail coverts and squarer tail shape. Plumage colours will certainly not identify it as an *Acrocephalus*. Marsh Warbler is closest, being more olive than russet in the mantle colour, but Booted looks much greyer. Garden Warbler is again confusable, particularly with Booted's shorter bill, but look for Booted Warbler's supercilium and markedly paler underparts.

Upcher's Warbler

PLATE 12

Hippolais languida (Hemprich and Ehrenberg)

FH. Hypolaïs d'Upcher   IT. Canapino languido
GR. Dombuschspötter

Breeding
Present in
summer only
Occurs regularly
on spring and
autumn migration

DISTRIBUTION AND HABITAT   Syria and Israel to Baluchistan and north to Caspian and Aral Sea. Eastwards to W. Tian Shan Mts. and Tadzhikistan. Migrates through Iraq, Iran, Arabia, and N.E. Africa to winter in E. Africa.

Frequents open arid areas, scrub, gardens, and vineyards. Bushes on mountain slopes up to 6000 ft.

DESCRIPTION   Length 5½ in (14 cm)

Brownish-grey upperparts with faint whitish supercilium and eye ring. Whitish underparts, suffused with pale buff on flanks and occasionally across the breast. Tail is dusky grey and contrasts clearly with paler grey rump. Outer half of outside tail feathers brownish-white, broadly tipped with clearer white. In autumn, adult's wing and tail feathers get very worn and look browner than those of first-winter birds. These show a

57

dull pale centre-wing panel similar to spring adults. Wings have well-marked, white feather-edges. Under-tail coverts may be slightly yellowish and tail itself only slightly rounded. Bill dark brown above, flesh-coloured below and noticeably long. Legs pale brown and iris light brown.

IN THE FIELD

Generally greyer in the field than Olivaceous Warbler, but barely identifiable. Wings of Upcher's are longer and more pointed. Typical *Hippolais* clumsy foraging action. Of all *Hippolais*, has the most prominent tail movement, flicking up and down and frequently cocking and opening it. Appears to have a longer tail than other *Hippolais*, but the high crown gives an impression of a *Sylvia* warbler. Upcher's stance is frequently reminiscent of a chat. First points to notice are pale brown legs, rump contrast with tail and tail-movements.

SONG

Call note is a unique monosyllable described as a loud 'chuck'. Also reported is a sharp double note 'tchik-tchik'. The alarm note is a low prolonged churring and song is acrocephaline in tone with more harsh notes than is usual with *Hippolais*.

SIMILAR SPECIES

The call is the major field difference between Upcher's and Olivaceous, but Upcher's tail movements are definitive if observed. The dark tail and contrasting pale rump is more marked in Upcher's than in any other *Hippolais*, though Olivaceous is nearest and care in differentiation is necessary.

Compared with Garden Warbler, Upcher's is less olive-brown and has white in the tail. The long wings and bill and flat forehead identify Upcher's readily as a *Hippolais*, but from then on certain identification needs considerable patience.

Olive Tree Warbler PLATE 17

Hippolais olivetorum (Strickland)

FH. Hypolaïs des oliviers   DU. Griekse spotvogel
IT. Canapino levantino   GR. Olivenspötter
SW. Olivgulsångare   SP. Zarcero grande

Breeding
Present in
summer only

DISTRIBUTION
AND HABITAT

S. Yugoslavia to Greece, Bulgaria, Turkey, Syria, N. Israel, and N. Iran. Also Crete and possibly Cyprus. Migrates to E. Africa from Kenya south to Transvaal.

Frequents thorn-scrub, olive and oak woods, scattered trees, and open woodlands and orchards.

DESCRIPTION

Length 6 in (15 cm)

Grey above tinged with brown, with slight whitish supercilium and eye ring. Underparts white suffused with pale yellow on breast and greyish tinge in flanks. A pale mid-wing panel persists in adults until about mid-June. Outer tail feathers have white margins and these and penultimate tail feathers have a white crescent at the tip. Bill is conspicuously long and heavy, dark brown above and yellowish below. Legs bluish-grey. Iris dark

59

brown. First-year birds are more olive above than adults and have a clearer, whiter mid-wing panel, though no yellow on underparts.

IN THE FIELD   Largest *Hippolais* warbler. Shy and skulking. Appears to be a clumsy, heavy, pale bird with a noticeably large bill, very long wings and tail, a pale eyestripe, and whitish borders to flight feathers and wing coverts, giving impression of dark grey and white stripes. Very shallow and inconspicuous tail-flicking movements.

SONG   Similar to Sedge Warbler in loudness, but more melodious and musical, almost thrush-like in quality. Deeper tone than other *Hippolais*' songs. More distinctive note than other *Hippolais* warblers—transcribed as a two-note 'trr-trrk', but other *Hippolais* may utter their single call notes in pairs with equal emphasis.

SIMILAR SPECIES   Size difference, greyness, and length of bill separate the Olive Tree Warbler from other *Hippolais* warblers fairly easily, but in size and general plumage tone, this bird closely resembles a first-winter Barred Warbler. Again greyness, heavier build, and large bill should identify Olive Tree Warbler. Barred Warbler has a longer tail and a smaller body and its pale supercilium does not extend behind its eye. Head shape and hawk-like expression of Barred Warbler are quite different.

Icterine Warbler

PLATE 18

Hippolais icterina (Vieillot)

FH. Hypolaïs ictérine DU. Spotvogel IT. Canapino maggiore
GR. Gelbspötter SW. Gulsångare SP. Zarcero icterino

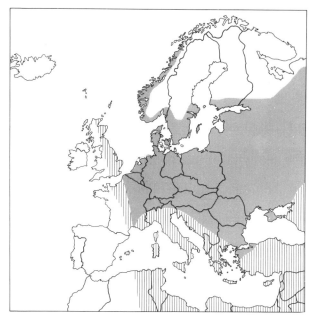

Breeding
Present in
summer only
Occurs regularly
on spring and
autumn migration

DISTRIBUTION AND HABITAT

Breeds from the Arctic Circle in Europe south to N. and E. France and N. Italy. Then eastwards to Ural Mts. and Russian Altai. There is also an isolated population in N. Iran.

Migrates to tropical and southern Africa in savannah woodland, gardens, and palm groves. Fairly regularly on passage in Britain, more commonly in autumn and mostly to east and south coasts.

Prefers sunny forest edges with broad-leaved trees. Often in damp areas. Also in orchards, parks, and gardens with clumps of trees. Generally found high up in tall, thickly-leaved trees.

DESCRIPTION

Length 5¼ in (13.5 cm)

Whole upperparts are uniform olive-brown and underparts all pale yellow. Sides of breast and flanks

61

have slightly brownish tinge. Short supercilium and eye ring are yellow. Wings and tail dark brown with outer pair of tail feathers narrowly and indistinctly bordered white. Fringes of secondaries and tertiaries golden yellow (or whitish in first-year birds) and, together with fringes of greater wing coverts, form a pale panel in the middle of the closed wing, in marked contrast to the remainder. This feature persists through migration period since the complete moult is usually after arrival at winter quarters. Adult in autumn plumage is generally greyer than in spring. Bill is relatively large and broad, dark brown above and flesh coloured below, with yellow along cutting edges. Legs are bluish grey; mouth is bright orange and iris dark brown. Sexes alike.

Juvenile is much paler olive-brown above and paler yellow below, the pale wing panel being less distinct than in the spring adult, but can be more distinct than the autumn adult which may have very abraded wing feathers.

IN THE FIELD

Active, lively, and excitable. Movements in foliage are heavy and deliberate compared to *Phylloscopus* warblers. Icterines spend most of their time in tree foliage and are often difficult to see clearly. Rarely seen on the ground. When excited or curious, they may raise crown feathers to give a large-headed impression. Flight is less hurried than in *Phylloscopus* warblers. Icterines usually reveal their presence by their peculiar song, but look particularly for peaked crown, prominent bill, and pale wing patch.

SONG

Normally heard after arrival at breeding ground and continues until after emergence of fledglings. Song is loud, vehement, and varied; a rich stream of musical notes, interspersed with sections of harsh chattering and discordant grating notes. Much repetition of both harsh and musical notes. Often highly imitative, and may sing at night. The call notes are a resonant, liquid 'di-di-oo-ee-oo', a harsh *Sylvia* like 'tek-tek' and a low growling 'churr' of alarm. In autumn it may give a soft 'hoo-eet' call, very similar to that of a Willow Warbler.

SIMILAR SPECIES

There may be confusion, not only with other genera, but with other *Hippolais* warblers. Compared with *Phylloscopus* warblers, Icterines are markedly larger and more stockily built. They sit more upright, and forage through the foliage with more deliberate, heavier movements than *Phylloscopus*. A prime characteristic (of all *Hippolais* warblers) is the way in which they stretch their necks upwards to reach a berry, then give a sharp tug of the head to pull it off. Compared with *Acrocephalus* warblers, Icterines are greener above and yellower below than any of them, and have longer wings and squarer tails. The only *Sylvia* warbler likely to be confusing is the Garden Warbler, but this has no supercilium, shorter wings, a rounder head, and a shorter narrower tail. The pale panel in the centre of the closed wing prevents confusion with any *Phylloscopus* or *Sylvia* warblers.

Compared with other *Hippolais* warblers, Melodious is the only other one with yellow underparts. Melodious are generally found in lower, thicker bushes than Icterines, and may also be seen on the ground occasionally. The Melodious Warbler's song is much less vehement and harsh and the call note is a soft sparrowlike twitter. Icterine has a longer, more pointed wing, noticeable both when flying or sitting. Additionally it retains its pale wing panel when seen in autumn, due to its late moult.

Occasionally Icterines occur in autumn with a very washed-out grey appearance, all the yellow having disappeared. They then become exceptionally difficult to identify and structure and voice must be relied on alone.

Melodious Warbler

PLATE 19

Hippolais polyglotta (Vieillot)

FH. Hypolaïs polyglotte   DU. Orpheusspotvogel
IT. Canapino   GR. Orpheusspötter
SW. Polyglottgulsångare   SP. Zarcero comun

Breeding
Present in
summer only
Occurs regularly
on spring and
autumn migration

DISTRIBUTION
AND HABITAT

France (except N. and E.), S. Tyrol, Italy, Iberian peninsula, and N. Africa from Morocco to Tunisia. Migrates to W. Africa, wintering to the west of Icterine Warbler, from Senegal to Cameroun. Regularly occurs in S. England. Found in a variety of woodland habitats, from dense growths of oak, alder, acacia, etc., to smaller trees and bushes along streams, ditches, and roadside verges. More rarely in gardens, until after breeding season.

DESCRIPTION

Length 5 in (13 cm)
    Characteristic contrast between brownish olive upperparts and rich yellow underparts. Very high crown gives it a 'capped' look. In spring, Melodious looks brighter than Icterine, but in autumn appears

more buffy below. The Melodious also has a pale wing panel, but it is never as conspicuous as the Icterine's, and has generally disappeared by mid-year. Legs bluish-grey to brown-grey. Bill broad, dark brown above and yellowish-flesh below. Mouth bright orange. Iris dark brown. Juveniles have no pale wing panel and are generally browner overall than adults. Occasionally both adults and juveniles lack yellow pigment and then look very washed out, buffy brown above and creamy white below.

IN THE FIELD Heavy, deliberate, clambering movements typical of the genus, but is frequently found at low levels in shrubs or bushes and occasionally on the ground. Generally shy, but shows itself when singing. Appears more compact and dumpy than Icterine. Melodious has a para-chute-like display flight, immediately reminiscent of a Tree Pipit (*Anthus trivialis*). Bill is relatively long and strong, but may appear to be less large than Icterine's because of Melodious' more rounded head. Look for contrasting olive above and yellow below, with short rounded wings and (in the autumn) no pale wing panel.

SONG Less vehement and more subdued than Icterine's, but also harsh. Rapid in delivery and can be imitative. Call note is a sparrow-like twitter, but on passage, Melo-dious also has a soft, Phylloscopine 'hoo-eet' almost indistinguishable from Icterine's autumn call. The song begins slowly then accelerates and contains sparrow-like chirping notes and mimicry, but with very little repetition.

SIMILAR SPECIES Birds with normal yellow pigment are confusable only with Icterine Warblers (see under Icterine Warbler).

Compared with *Phylloscopus* warblers, Melodious is larger and heavier with a longer, stronger bill, and a high crown. Compared with yellow, first-year Willow Warblers in autumn, Melodious has a sharper contrast between yellow underparts and dark olive-brown upperparts.

Compared with Icterine Warbler, voice is most distinctive difference. Visually Melodious has noticeably shorter wings, not extending beyond the base of the tail and clearly seen when sitting or flying. Generally somewhat browner upperparts than Icterine Warbler and legs also are browner. When yellow pigment is lacking, Melodious Warblers can be confused with Olivaceous Warblers, but are without any white in the tail. Melodious' fluttering flight is very similar to Olivaceous.

Marmora's Warbler

PLATE 20

Sylvia sarda Temminck

FH. Fauvette sarde   DU. Sardijnse
IT. Magnanina sarda   GR. Sardengrasmücke
SW. Sardinisk sångare   SP. Curraca sarda

Breeding
Present through-
out the year
Occurs in
winter

DISTRIBUTION
AND HABITAT

Confined to western Mediterranean area, specifically
N.E. Spain, Corsica, Sardinia, S. Sicily, coastal Tunisia,
and Balearic Is. Mainly sedentary but may wander in
winter to the northern edge of the Sahara, and is a
vagrant in S. Spain, Italy, and Malta.

Habitat is exactly similar to that of Dartford Warbler,
rough ground, with heather or gorse. Always dry,
bushy localities often in rocky country. Where both
Dartford and Marmora's occur together, Marmora's is
usually found in more mountainous country.

DESCRIPTION

Length 4¾ in (12 cm)

Male upperparts very dark blue-grey, washed with
dark brown. Underparts paler blue-grey. Chin and
throat feathers have white tips and centre of belly is

white. Slight pinkish tinge on flanks. Wings are dark brown and inner secondaries and greater coverts have rufous margins. Tail is long, blackish-brown, with the four outer tail feathers outlined in dirty white. Female is browner on upperparts and underparts with grey restricted to breast and lower throat. Belly and flanks are dull pinkish-brown.

Immatures are paler brown above and whiter below than adults.

Bill is dark horn with base of lower mandible flesh coloured. Legs yellowish-brown. Iris yellowish-brown with eye ring dull red. Mouth orange-yellow.

Race in the Balearic Is. is separated as *S. s. balearica*, and is slightly smaller with stronger pinkish wash on the lower breast.

IN THE FIELD
Behaviour very similar to Dartford Warbler. Very secretive, diving from bush to bush and very difficult to see for any length of time. Weak flight with long tail making the bird look unbalanced. Always looks very dark.

SONG
Call is a distinctive 'tsiig' uttered sharply or rapidly repeated as an alarm rattle. Song similar to Dartford's but less harsh, softer, and generally weaker. Notes sound more slurred than those of Dartford.

SIMILAR SPECIES
Can only be confused with Dartford Warbler, being the same size and distinctive shape, but the slate grey underparts of Marmora's are an important field mark and it is browner on wings and tail, and paler from centre of breast to undertail coverts. Immature Marmora's is paler and greyer above and much whiter below than immature Dartford Warbler.

Dartford Warbler

PLATE 20

Sylvia undata (Boddaert)

FH. Fauvette pitchou   DU. Provence-grasmus
IT. Magnanina   GR. Provencegrasmücke
SW. Provence-sångare   SP. Curraca rabilarga

Breeding
Present through-
out the year

Occurs in
winter

DISTRIBUTION
AND HABITAT

From southern England, W. France and Iberian peninsula east to Italy and south to N.W. Africa. Mainly
sedentary.

Favours thick cover in the maquis or other scrub-
covered regions and on bracken-covered heaths, rough
land, or any area with heather, furze, or gorse.

DESCRIPTION

Length 5 in (12.5 cm)

Male upperparts dull chocolate brown, head and nape
more slaty grey, especially in late summer. Ear coverts
and sides of neck also grey with white moustachial
stripes. Throat feathers have small white tips against
dark purplish-brown ground. Flanks are dirty brown
and centre of belly whitish. Undertail coverts brownish
grey with white feather fringes. Wings are very dark

69

brown with tertials and greater coverts broadly fringed with rufous. Tail is black with outer pair of feathers having dull white tips. Female is slightly paler and whole effect is much drabber than male.

Immature birds have buffish throat and breast.

Bill is dark brown with base of lower mandible yellowish. Legs are pale buff to brownish-yellow. Eye ring brown to orange red. Gape yellow.

IN THE FIELD

A highly secretive bird, only fleetingly seen as it flies low from one bush to another. Its small size, dark coloration, and very long dark tail, often cocked and fanned out, are distinctive. It has a weak flight, usually keeping close to the ground, with its long tail bobbing up and down in top-heavy fashion. When perched the tail is usually flicked frequently.

SONG

Call note is a grating, metallic 'churr', a short, hard 'tuk' or a combination of both 'churr-tuk-tuk' becoming a fast rattling repetition when alarmed. Song is a short musical chatter, often given in a dancing display flight, but frequently repeated interspersed with more liquid notes. Song is reminiscent of a Whitethroat's, but more mellow and bubbling, and is noticeably slower in delivery than that of a Sardinian Warbler.

SIMILAR
SPECIES

Shape, habitat, and voice make this bird unmistakeable from all others except the very similar Marmora's Warbler, with which it may occur. Notice Dartford's reddish breast. Marmora's looks darker still than Dartford. Dartford gives an overall dark brown impression, whilst Marmora's looks a more overall grey.

Spectacled Warbler

PLATE 21

Sylvia conspicillata Temminck

FH. Fauvette à lunettes (masquée)   DU. Brilgrasmus
IT. Sterpazzola di Sardegna   GR. Brillengrasmücke
SW. Glasögonsångare   SP. Curruca tomillera

Breeding
Present in
summer only

Breeding
Present through-
out the year

Occurs in
winter

DISTRIBUTION
AND HABITAT

Cape Verde Is., Madeira, Canary Is., and W. Mediterranean basin and its islands. East as far as Italy and Tunisia. Also occurs in Israel, Jordan, and possible N.E. Egypt, but does not occur in E. Europe. Partially a migrant, wintering just south of the breeding range, in Saharan oases, Egypt and on passage in Cyprus. Accidental to Britain.

Inhabits dry localities, particularly *Salicornia* and other low bushes. Often on coastal flats and in scrub, and may be seen associating with Dartford Warbler in gorse and heather environment. Appears never to favour tall shrubs or trees.

DESCRIPTION

Length 5 in (12.5 cm)
Male has crown and forehead pale grey, nape and

71

back of crown browner. Back rich brown, lower back and rump grey brown. Throat white turning to grey towards breast. Upper breast pink, sides and flanks brownish-pink, paler towards centre of belly and under-tail coverts. Occasionally moustachial stripes are prominently white, but not always. Wings and tail dark brown with broad chestnut tips to coverts. Outer tail feathers white, penultimate feathers tipped white. Females are browner on the head than males. Throat is suffused buff and sides and flanks rufous-buff. There is a conspicuous chestnut patch on the female's wing. Immature resemble females but are browner and have no grey at all.

Bill dark horn, yellowish along cutting edge and at base of lower mandible. Legs are reddish brown in spring, turning pale yellowish in autumn. Iris variable from yellowish-brown to reddish-orange. Eye ring whitish.

The race in Madeira and Cape Verde Is., *S. c. orbitalis*, is generally darker grey-brown above and less rufous than European race, but can be very variable, particularly in Madeira.

IN THE FIELD

Resembles a small dark-headed Whitethroat or possibly a washed-out looking Subalpine Warbler. Very obvious white throat. Head of male with dark back and tail and especially chestnut edges to wing coverts are best field marks. Note also in autumn the pale, straw-coloured legs. Narrow white eye ring is difficult to see.

SONG

Alarm call is a rattling 'kerr' and recalls a Wren (*T. troglodytes*), but more subdued. Song is a short, high-pitched warble, pleasant and musical and without grating notes. Somewhat deliberate, monotonous phrases, uttered from an exposed twig or in a dancing song flight.

SIMILAR SPECIES

Adult male birds may be confused with Whitethroat, Lesser Whitethroat, and Subalpine Warblers. Spectacled is generally darker than Whitethroat and slightly smaller. Head particularly is darker, throat whiter, legs paler, and eye ring white. It has a more distinctive chestnut wing patch and darker grey line through the eye. A less strident or scratchy song further distinguishes Spectacled. Spectacled's head is similar to Lesser Whitethroat, but it is again a generally darker bird. Chestnut wing patch is not present in Lesser Whitethroat.

Compared with Subalpine Warblers, Spectacled's rufous wings, white throat, and paler breast are diagnostic. Subalpine is usually much redder on the breast and moustachial stripes more obvious.

A detailed study of the differences between females and immatures of Spectacled Warbler and other *Sylvia* Warblers has been made by J. T. R. Sharrock (1962 *British Birds* **55,** 90–2). From this and other documentation, I have constructed the key on page 74. See also J. J. Swift (1959 *British Birds* **52,** 198–9).

Chart of differences between various *Sylvia* Warblers (females and immatures)

	Spectacled	Subalpine	Sardinian	White-throat	Lesser White-throat
General appearance	Neat	Neat and small	Long-tailed, bulky, heavy	Bulky	Neat
Crown	Darkish grey	Grey	Very dark grey	Grey	Dark grey
Ear coverts	Not dark	Not dark	Dark	Not dark	Dark
Rufous in wing	Yes	No	No	Yes	No
Orange wash on flanks	Yes	Yes	No	No	No
Eye ring	White (inconspicuous)	Reddish (not immature)	Red	Dark	Dark
Tail movements	Cocks regularly	Cocks regularly	Cocks and and fans regularly	Spreads but rarely cocks it	Not cocked regularly

Subalpine Warbler

PLATE 22

Sylvia cantillans (Pallas)

FH. Fauvette passerinette   DU. Baardgrasmus
IT. Sterpazzolina   GR. Weissbartgrasmücke
SW. Rödstrupig sångare   SP. Curruca carrasquena

Breeding
Present in
summer only
Occurs regularly
on spring and
autumn migration

DISTRIBUTION
AND HABITAT

Breeds in S. Europe from Iberian peninsula eastwards to Asia Minor and Syria. Also in N.W. Africa. Mainly migratory, moving across Mediterranean and N. Africa to winter south of Sahara desert, eastward to Lake Chad. Scarce autumn vagrant to Britain.

Thorny and xerophytic scrub on arid hillsides. Low bushes and thickets, often with scattered trees. Open woodland; moist, shady localities, thick undergrowth, hedgerows, and streamside vegetation.

DESCRIPTION

Length 4¾ in (12 cm)

Upperparts of male are bluish-grey with tinge of dark brown, especially on upper back. Ear coverts brownish. Small chestnut supercilium and pronounced white moustachial stripes. Chin, throat, and breast are

75

pinkish-chestnut to dark terracotta extending down flanks, leaving centre of belly and undertail coverts whitish washed with brownish-pink. Wings are dark brown, as is tail, but three outer rectrices show some white. Female is browner above and much whiter below than male. Females vary in brightness of underparts and brighter ones show also very clearly white moustachial stripes.

Autumn immature males are similar to adults. Immature females are olive-brown on mantle with head greyish-brown and nape greyer. Chin and throat are white, flushed with buff. Sides of breast and flanks are brownish-orange and centre of belly whiter. White parts of tail feathers are smudged with brown.

Bill is dark horn, purplish at base of lower mandible. Legs are pale brown or yellowish. Iris is pale brown. Eye ring is bright red in males, variably red to brown in females and dull gold in immatures.

The N. African sedentary race, *S. c. inornata* is similar but lacks pinkish tone of nominate race, *S. c. cantillans*.

The race in S.E. Europe *S. c. albistriata*, which is a partial migrant to W. Africa is browner above and whiter below than *S. c. cantillans*. The breast colour is mostly brown, and there is less colour on sides and flanks. The white moustachial stripes are mostly broader and there may be white tips to throat and breast feathers.

IN THE FIELD

Resembles small pale Dartford Warbler, with which it occurs. A small, delicate bird with noticeably long tail. Appears to be pale grey above and buffish pink below. Mostly skulking in behaviour and characteristically raises and spreads tail, particularly when alarmed. In flight the tail is square-ended and the white of the outer feathers is noticeable. Can appear short-necked on occasions.

SONG

Alarm-note is a hard but quiet 'tek-tek' frequently repeated, and a quick chattering buzz. The song is delivered from exposed points in bushes and during the brief, dancing song-flight. Similar to that of Sardinian Warbler or to Whitethroat's, but is slower than Sardinian's and more musical and sustained than Whitethroat's and without the harsh, rattling notes.

Habitat and behaviour are similar to Dartford Warbler's, but Subalpine is smaller, paler and the tail,
although long, is much shorter than Dartford's.

Subalpine is separated from Spectacled Warbler by its
oranger underparts and wings being grey-brown rather
than pale brown.

Compared with Ménétries' Warbler, Subalpine has
red eye ring and a paler head.

For differences and similarities between female and
immatures of Subalpine Warbler, compared to other
Sylvia warblers, see chart on page 74.

Ménétries' Warbler

PLATE 23

Sylvia mystacea Ménétries

FH. Fauvette de Ménétries   IT. Bigia di Ménétries
GR. Östliche Samtkopfgrasmücke   SP. Curraca de Ménétries

Breeding
Present in
summer only
Occurs regularly
on spring and
autumn migration

**DISTRIBUTION
AND HABITAT**

S. Russia from Lower Volga River to N. Caucasus, Transcaucasia, Iraq, Jordan, and Israel. From Afghanistan and Iran north to Aral Sea and Tadzikistan. Migrates to S. Arabia and N.E. Africa from Egypt to Somalia. Almost unknown in W. Europe.

Plains and lower mountain slopes. Commonly in shrubs, principally tamarisks, but often in rocky areas and river valleys.

DESCRIPTION

Length 5 in (13 cm)

Upperparts dark grey, often brownish on nape and upper mantle. Crown, forehead, and ear coverts dull blackish-brown blending into dark nape. Underparts vary from white with faint pinkish flush on breast and flanks to dirty white with much stronger terracotta on throat, upper breast, and flanks. These latter birds have white chins and moustachial stripes. Undertail coverts are grey with long, white fringes reaching well down tail. Wings and tail dark brown and well rounded tail has outer feathers and tips of next two inwards white. Female is greyish-brown above with rusty brown forehead and underparts whitish with buffish tinge on breast and brownish flanks.

Immature similar to female, but has pinkish wash on breast.

Bill brownish, base of lower mandible pale straw. Legs light reddish-brown or flesh coloured. Eye varies from light brown to reddish-brown, and eye ring pale orange to pale brick red, but generally less red than Sardinian Warbler's.

IN THE FIELD
Similar in appearance to Sardinian Warbler with which it may in fact be conspecific. Geographically it replaces Sardinian Warbler in the lower Volga basin. Behaviour is similar, but Ménétries is even more restless and active and tends to remain deep inside bushes. Gives impression of somewhat washed-out Sardinian Warbler. In flight tail is carried noticeably high. Look for buffy-pink underparts.

SONG
Call is a sharply repeated 'tat' and a rattling double note when alarmed. The song is said to be similar to that of Whitethroat, but is more musical and varied and with fewer harsh notes.

SIMILAR SPECIES
Sardinian warbler, particularly the paler Near East race S. m. momus. Moustachial stripes may be more evident in Ménétries and in both male and female Ménétries are paler on flanks and normally have redder legs. Female Ménétries is normally browner than female Sardinian with less grey on the head; but Ménétries remains highly variable over its range and great care is necessary to identify it correctly.

Sardinian Warbler

PLATE 23

Sylvia melanocephala (Gmelin)

FH. Fauvette mélanocéphale DU. Kleine zwartkop
IT. Occhiocotto GR. Samtkopfgrasmücke
SW. Sammetshätta SP. Curruca cabecinegra

Breeding
Present in
summer only

Occurs regularly
on spring and
autumn migration

Breeding
Present through-
out the year

Occurs in
winter

DISTRIBUTION AND HABITAT

All of Mediterranean basin and its islands. Normally sedentary but occasionally individuals winter in Sahara desert, northern Iraq and Arabia. Accidental to Britain.

Characteristic bird of Mediterranean scrub. In open woodland with thick undergrowth and in bushes and thickets in mountainous country. Also in olive groves, vineyards, parks, gardens, and in urban areas.

DESCRIPTION

Length 5¼ in (13.5 cm)

Male has dark grey mantle suffused with dark brown. Head is glossy black to below the eye. Chin and throat are white and remainder of underparts washed pale grey, darker on the flanks. Wings are dark brown and tail darker with white on three outer feathers, whitest on the outermost. Female is brown with grey on rump and a greyish head. Occasionally has some black on the crown. Underparts are white with a buffish tinge on sides, flanks, and breast. Undertail coverts are brown with broad white fringes and the tail itself blackish-brown, darker than the wings as in the male. Immature males are browner on the crown, nape, and back than adults, but can be widely variable. Wings and tail are browner and white area on tail is dirtier than adult colours. Immature females have very little grey on the head and rump, the head being the same colour as the mantle and the white in the tail is again a dirty grey.

Bill black with base of lower mandible pale horn. Legs olive-brown or may be paler. Iris reddish and eye ring bright crimson with a ring of feathers pale pink in adults and pinkish-brown in immatures.

IN THE FIELD   A restless perky and inquisitive bird. Very lively and active but given to skulking. Solid black cap of male and clearly visible red eye ring of both adults are characteristic. In flight the bird is usually identified by the conspicuous white outer tail feathers, but deliberate wing beats and bobbing flight are also important points. Also clearly seen in flight are white markings on undertail coverts and relatively long wings and tail. Tail is graduated and frequently cocked and may be spread, even in flight. Crown feathers may be raised as tail is cocked.

SONG   Call note is a hard, typically *Sylvia* 'teck-teck', and a harsh alarm rattle, a fast stuttering 'ti-ti-ti-tick' said to resemble the winding of a clock. Song is somewhat similar to Whitethroat's but is longer, more musical and interspersed with phrases of the harsh alarm note. The song may be given from both exposed or hidden perches and in the brief, dancing song flight.

SIMILAR
SPECIES   Superficially resembles several *Sylvia* warblers, but in its habitat is by far the commonest of this group. Females and immatures may easily be confused with other *Sylvia* warblers, but their differences and similarities are set out in the chart on page 74.

Compared with Blackcap, male is separated by black cap extending to below the eye, the red eye ring and general behaviour. Female Sardinian is more monocoloured than female Blackcap and white tail feathers are distinctive.

Orphean Warbler is much larger and has a very noticeable pale eye, though the white outer tail feathers may cause confusion.

Rüppell's Warbler female may also be confused with Sardinian, and here the white moustachial streak and mottled throat of Rüppell's should be enough to separate it.

Cetti's Warbler

PLATE I

imm.

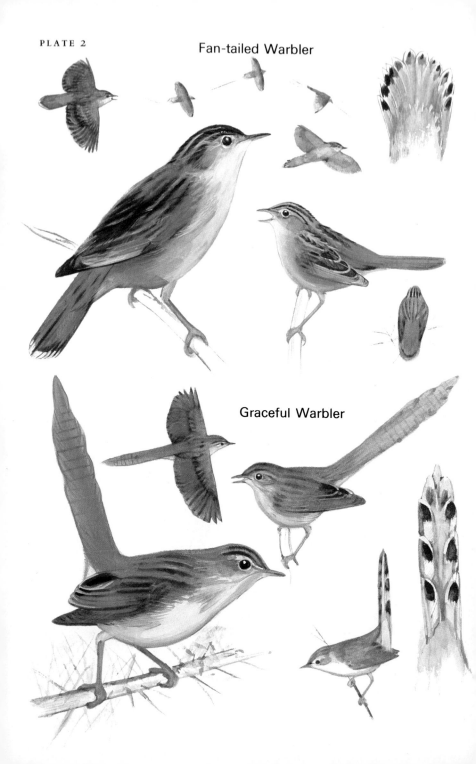

PLATE 2

Fan-tailed Warbler

Graceful Warbler

PLATE 3

Green Warbler

imm.

Scrub Warbler

Dusky
Warbler
ad.

① ②

imm.
in autumn
plumage

① ②

skulking

Gray's Grasshopper
Warbler

PLATE 4

Pallas' Grasshopper Warbler

imm.

PLATE 5

Lanceolated Warbler
various ad.

PLATE 6

Grasshopper Warbler
ad. various views

Yellow phase

River Warbler
various ad.

PLATE 7

PLATE 8

Savi's Warbler
all ad. various views

PLATE 9

Moustached Warbler

imm.

PLATE 10

Garden Warbler

ad.

ad.

imm.

Aquatic Warbler

ad.

ad.

PLATE II

Sedge Warbler

imm.

PLATE 12

Radde's Warbler

imm. in autumn

Booted Warbler

imm. in autumn

Upcher's Warblers

Paddyfield
Warbler

in autumn

Blyth's Reed Warbler
various ad.

PLATE 13

ad.

imm.

Marsh Warbler

ad.

imm.

imm.

PLATE 14

Reed Warbler

autumn
ad.

Great Reed Warbler

PLATE 15

ad.

ad.

ad.

ad.

ad.

Thick-billed
Warbler

PLATE 16

Olivaceous Warbler

ad.

ad.

imm.
autumn

ad.

ad.

ad.

Olive-tree Warbler

PLATE 17

ad.

ad.

1st winter

ad.

ad.

PLATE 18

ad.

ad.

Icterine Warbler

imm. in
autumn

ad.

brown phase

PLATE 19

Melodious Warbler

ad.

ad.

imm.
autumn

ad.

ad.

brown phase

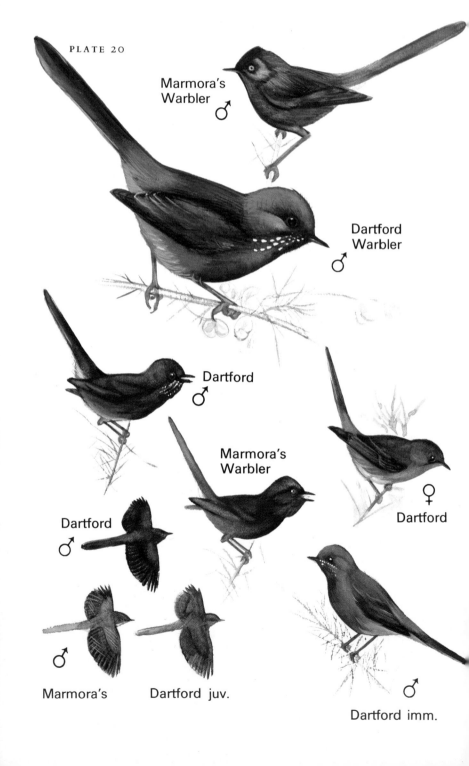

PLATE 20

Marmora's Warbler ♂

Dartford Warbler ♂

Dartford ♂

Marmora's Warbler

Dartford ♀

Dartford ♂

Marmora's

Dartford juv.

Dartford imm. ♂

PLATE 21

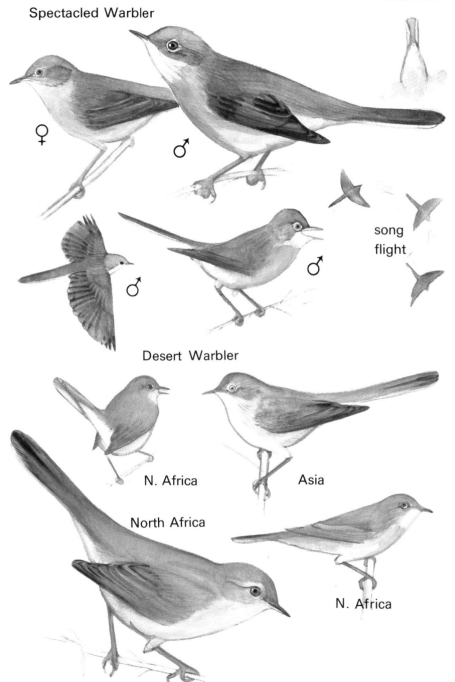

Spectacled Warbler

♀

♂

♂

song flight

♂

Desert Warbler

N. Africa

Asia

North Africa

N. Africa

PLATE 22

Subalpine Warbler

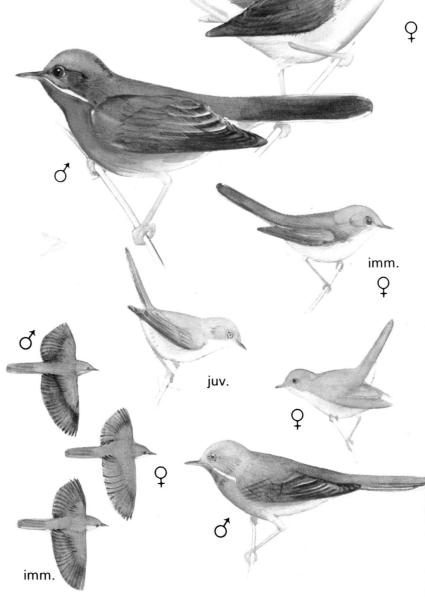

♀

♂

imm.
♀

♂

juv.

♀

♂

♀

imm.

PLATE 23

Ménétries' Warbler ♂

Sardinian Warbler ♂

Sardinian ♀

Sardinian

Sardinian ♂

Cyprus Warbler ♂

Sardinian ♂

Ménétries' ♂

PLATE 24

Rüppell's Warblers

Blackcaps

PLATE 25

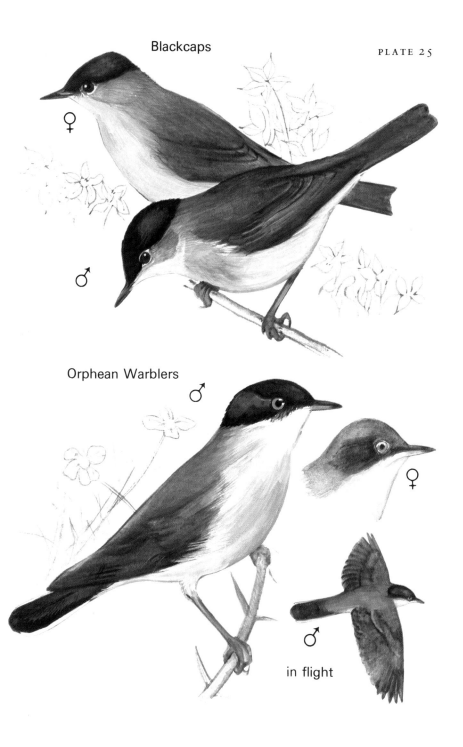

♀

♂

Orphean Warblers

♂

♀

♂

in flight

PLATE 26

Barred Warbler

♂

Shrike-like
posture

♀

imm.

♂

♂

imm.

PLATE 27

Lesser Whitethroat

ad.

ad.

imm.

imm.

Whitethroat

♂

♀

imm.

PLATE 28

ad.

Greenish Warbler

autumn
ad.

imm.

Arctic Warbler

ad.

autumn
ad.

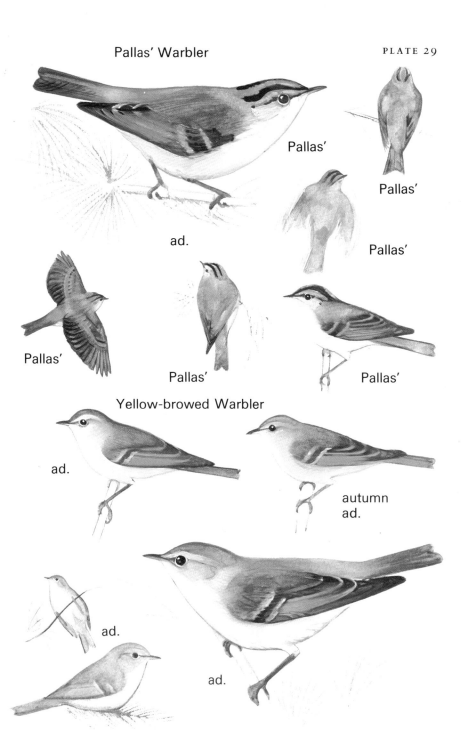

Pallas' Warbler

PLATE 29

Pallas'

Pallas'

ad.

Pallas'

Pallas'

Pallas'

Pallas'

Yellow-browed Warbler

ad.

autumn
ad.

ad.

ad.

PLATE 30

Wood Warbler

ad.

display

Bonelli's Warbler
All ad.

autumn
ad.

Willow Warbler

PLATE 31

imm.

ad.

imm.

ad.

imm.

Chiffchaff

ad.

Northern
Chiffchaff

imm.

PLATE 32

Goldcrest

Goldcrest juv.

♂

Firecrest

♂

Firecrest

Goldcrest juv.

Goldcrest

Firecrest

Goldcrest

Gold-crest

Firecrest juv.

Firecrest

Firecrest

Goldcrest

♀ ♂

Firecrest

♀ ♂

Cyprus Warbler

PLATE 23

Sylvia melanothorax Tristram

FH. Fauvette mélanocéphale de Chypre   IT. Bigia di Cipro
GR. Zypernsamtkopfgrasmücke

DISTRIBUTION
AND HABITAT

Confined to Cyprus. In winter may wander to Israel and Lebanon. May be found in orange groves, reed beds or any scrub area from the coast up to 6000 ft. Occasionally found in woodlands.

DESCRIPTION

Length 5¼ in (13.5 cm)
 This bird is closely allied to Rüppell's, Sardinian, and Ménétries Warblers, and has been placed within one of these variously by a number of authors. Williamson (1964) believed that however closely the Cyprus Warbler may have been connected at one time, it now stands as a valid species.
 Male has upperparts brownish grey with black crown and lores, bordered by a pronounced white moustachial stripe. Underparts are mottled black and white. Throat and upper breast are black with some white feather tips and lower breast and belly are black with more numerous and broader white feather edges. Flanks are pale grey washed with pink and some birds have a pinkish flush on the lower breast. Wings are blackish brown with dull white feather edges. Tail is black with outer two feathers largely white.
 Female is a mid-brown colour above with the head darker, occasionally mottled with black, but much less than on the male. Most of belly and breast are greyish-white with flanks a darker grey.
 Immature is a uniform dark brown.
 Bill is blackish above, greyish-horn below tipped with black. Legs are blackish-horn and eye ring bright, brick red with outer ring of white feathers and a chestnut iris.

IN THE FIELD

Habits and behaviour are very similar to Sardinian Warbler's; restless, skulking in thick cover, and constantly uttering its harsh call notes. Habitually cocks up tail to right angle with body. Generally very dark

appearance with striking white tail feathers and noticeably short wings.

SONG

Call note is a constantly repeated 'szack', uttered more
rapidly as an alarm note. Also a double call 'zigg-zigg',
lighter and quieter. Song is varied, somewhat like
Whitethroat's and delivered from the top of a bush or
small tree.

SIMILAR
SPECIES

Broad white edges to primaries and silvery white lower
belly distinguishes male Cyprus from Sardinian, but
females in autumn and winter are virtually impossible to
separate. In early spring, female Cyprus Warbler de-
velops faint crescent-shaped markings on the throat.
Even the calls are very similar, Cyprus perhaps has a
more sibilant and slightly less hard note.

Rüppell's Warbler

PLATE 24

Sylvia rueppelli Temminck

FH. Fauvette masquée   DU. Rüppell's grasmus
IT. Bigia di Rüppell   GR. Maskengrasmücke
SW. Svarthaked sångare   SP. Curraca de Rüppell

Breeding
Present in
summer only
Occurs regularly
on spring and
autumn migration

DISTRIBUTION
AND HABITAT

Greece, Crete, Aegean Is., Turkey, Lebanon, and Israel. Winters in N.E. Africa as far south as central Sudan. May also breed in Cyprus where it occurs on passage.

Thick scrub and low thorny bushes in rocky area. In winter in hedges, gardens and any low, tangled vegetation.

DESCRIPTION

Length $5\frac{1}{2}$ in (14 cm)

Male is grey on the upperparts, brownish-grey on the mantle. Head and throat are completely black with very conspicuous, thin, white, moustachial streaks. Rest of underparts creamy white with slight pink wash, centre of belly white and flanks pinkish-grey. Wings are black except for greyish-white feather tips and tail is also black with prominent, white, outer tail feathers. Female

85

has mottled instead of black throat, and a greyish-brown crown mottled with black. Moustachial streaks again prominent.

Immature males have browner crowns than adult males, and the grey of the upperparts is browner. Generally duller.

Bill is brownish-black above and lower mandible has a light brown base. Legs are bright reddish-brown and iris dull orange, with an orange-red eye ring.

IN THE FIELD

Best field marks are completely black head and throat of male and mottled throat of female. Also white moustachial streaks and reddish legs of both adults. Behaviour normally skulking but usually sings from an exposed perch.

SONG

Call and scolding notes are very similar to those of Sardinian Warbler, but louder and harsher and occasionally the scold finishes with a soft 'pit-pit'. Song is not as hurried as Sardinian's and is fuller and more musical. Song flight is very high and twisting.

SIMILAR SPECIES

Voice and appearance of female may be easily confused with Sardinian female, but moustachial streak and red legs should determine Rüppell's. Whilst song is not as rapid as Sardinian's, it is faster than Dartford's, with which it may also be confused. In flight, silhouette looks heavier than Sardinian, and when perched, Rüppell's is said to give impression of a convex back compared to Sardinian's concave appearance. Tail is shorter and squarer than Sardinian and mantle looks paler grey colour.

Desert Warbler

PLATE 21

Sylvia nana (Hemprich and Ehrenberg)

FH. Fauvette naine   IT. Sterpazzola nana
GR. Wustengrasmücke   SP. Curraca sahariana

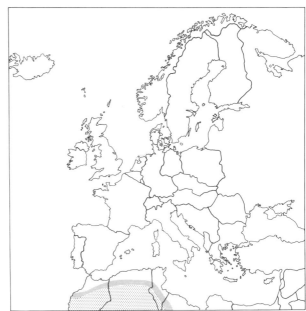

Breeding
Present in
summer only

Breeding
Present through-
out the year

DISTRIBUTION
AND HABITAT

Aral–Caspian region to Sinkiang and central Mongolia, south to S.E. Iran, Baluchistan, and W. Afghanistan. Winters in Egypt, Somalia, Arabia east to Pakistan, and N.W. India. Also northern fringe of Sahara desert from Morocco to Tripoli, migratory southwards. Accidentally to Italy and Madeira.

Confined to desert and semidesert localities including scrub and Acacia patches.

DESCRIPTION

Length 4½ in (11 cm)

Upperparts greyish sandy-brown with rump and uppertail coverts warmer sandy-buff. Small grey area around eye. Underparts creamy with buffy flanks and yellowish-buff belly and undertail coverts. Wings and tail darker brown with white on three outermost pairs

87

of tail feathers. Sexes similar. Immatures tinged more rufous on upperparts.

Bill yellowish with dark tip. Legs straw–yellow. Eye yellow with white eye ring.

N. African race, *S. n. deserti*, is very different from the nominate race in Asia, described above. *S. n. deserti* has upperparts pale sandy yellow with rufous uppertail coverts and underparts much purer white. Bill is pale flesh coloured; legs pale yellow and iris bright yellow.

IN THE FIELD   Normally stays well hidden in bushes, then flies low over the ground from one patch of scrub to another. Unmistakeable, even on the most fleeting sighting. No other bird of this general colour lives in Desert Warbler's biotope. On close sighting, yellow legs, bill, and eye are very noticeable.

SONG   Call is a short trill and song is a series of repeated low 'tee' notes. Several other song phrases of some variety have been reported, including a rich Whitethroat-like sequence.

SIMILAR   Garden Warbler has similar lack of distinguishing marks,
SPECIES   but Desert Warbler is much smaller and yellower.

Smaller and paler than Whitethroat or Spectacled, and lacks dark cheeks and eyes of Spectacled Warbler.

Other species cannot normally be confused with Desert Warbler.

Orphean Warbler

PLATE 25

Sylvia hortensis (Gmelin)

FH. Fauvette orphée   DU. Orphensgrasmus
IT. Bigia grossa   GR. Orpheusgrasmücke
SW. Mästersångare   SP. Curraca mirlona

Breeding
Present in
summer only
Occurs regularly
on spring and
autumn migration

DISTRIBUTION
AND HABITAT

Southern Europe from France to the Balkans and east across Iran and Russian Turkestan to N.W. India. Also N. Africa from Morocco to Libya. Migrates to Africa south of the Sahara, Sudan, and Egypt. Also to Arabia and S. India.

Found in open woodland with undergrowth; in orchards, parks and gardens with larger bushes and small trees; in olive, cork, ilex, and oak groves or plantations. In winter in riverside scrub and acacia scrub on desert fringes.

DESCRIPTION

Length 6 in (15 cm)

Male has dark grey mantle in spring turning olive-brown by autumn. Crown is dull black, darker in spring than autumn, which merges with mantle colour

89

at the nape. Underparts are white at chin, throat, and centre of belly and the remainder whitish with a pinkish-buff wash, darker on the flanks. Wings and tail are greyish-brown, the wing feathers narrowly edged with dirty white and the tail feathers (except centre pair) have white tips. Outermost tail feathers are almost totally white. Female has a browner mantle and a brown crown. Wings and tail are also browner than male's. Pink is less evident on underparts and buff more so.

Immatures have browner crowns than adult females.

Bill is black above, bluish grey and black-tipped below. Legs are bluish-black or slate-grey. Iris is pale yellow, appearing almost white, and the gape has a bluish colour.

As the populations range farther east, the general coloration becomes paler, except for the male crown colour which becomes blacker and more extensive in area. The clinal variation is slight and within the European boundaries there is very little difference in the population.

IN THE FIELD

Resembles a large stout Blackcap, but most noticeable are Orphean's white outer tail feathers, white eye, and white throat. Black cap extends down below eye. Typical *Sylvia* warbler behaviour, keeping well hidden, uttering scolding notes or giving its loud, thrush-like song from an exposed perch. Large size is good first clue to identity.

SONG

Call is a Blackcap-like 'tack-tack' and the alarm a harsh rattle. The song is loud and vigorous and the lack of harsh notes recalls a thrush. The phrases are often repeated four or five times giving a monotonous quality to the song which is its best identification feature.

SIMILAR
SPECIES

Blackcap is smaller, lacks white throat and pale eye of Orphean, and male has cap which does not extend below the eye.

Sardinian Warbler is also smaller and has a reddish rather than a pale eye. Habitats are normally very different.

Barred Warbler, immature, may be confused, but Orphean has a shorter tail and the uppertail coverts lack white tips.

Barred Warbler

PLATE 26

Sylvia nisoria (Bechstein)

FH. Fauvette épervière   DU. Gestreepte grasmus
IT. Bigia padovana   GR. Sperbergrasmücke
SW. Höksångare   SP. Curraca gavilana

Breeding
Present in
summer only
Occurs regularly
on spring and
autumn migration

DISTRIBUTION
AND HABITAT

S. Sweden, S. Finland, and central Russia south to N.E. France, N. Italy, and Bulgaria eastwards to Russian Turkestan, S.W. Mongolia, Sinkiang, and N. Iran. Migrates to eastern side of Africa, as far south as Natal and Zimbabwe. Regular but scarce autumn visitor to Britain.

Open country with shrubs and hedges, thorny thickets, bushy common or heathland, clearings in woodland. Also young plantations and parkland. In winter in thorny scrub and arid bush country.

DESCRIPTION

Length 6 in (15 cm)

Male upperparts brownish-grey with rump, uppertail coverts and some scapulars barred dark grey and tipped buffish white. Sides of crown are flecked with white and

91

ear coverts are grey-brown. Underparts are white with dark grey bars on sides of breast and flanks. Undertail coverts are grey-brown with broad white fringes. Wings are dark brown with narrow greyish-white fringes and two dull, white wingbars. Tail is dark grey-brown with most of the outer rectrices white, and the remainder (except for central pair) fringed white and with a white spot near the tip. Female is browner on the upperparts and less barred on the underparts than the male. The white tips to the tail feathers are narrower than on the male.

Juveniles are unbarred except for faint traces on the undertail coverts. They are sandier above than the adults, whiter below, and show a clearer wingbar.

Bill is dark brown with base of lower mandible yellowish. Legs are dull yellowish. Iris is bright yellow in adults, but dark in juveniles, only becoming pale the following spring.

IN THE FIELD

A large robust, long-tailed warbler recalling a Whitethroat in both shape and actions. Appears to have a fierce facial expression and raises crown and jerks tail when excited. Heavy appearance, noticeably stout legs and bill. Normal behaviour is skulking, but when seen the best field marks are the grey coloration, large size, and in adults, the barring and bright eye. Often associates with, and nests close to Red-backed Shrike (*Lanius collurio*).

SONG

Call note is usually a hard 'tack' and a distinctive grating 'tscharr-tscharr', which also can occur in the song. The song is delivered from a perch or in a short dancing display flight. It is similar to that of a Garden Warbler, but has a more rapid delivery, shorter phrases and contains more harsh notes. Song frequently begins and ends with the grating chatter.

SIMILAR SPECIES

Adult male is distinctive amongst all European birds, but females and immatures may be confusing. They are distinguished from Whitethroat and Garden Warbler by greyer appearance, wingbars and larger size. Young shrikes may also be confused, but again wingbars and white on tail feathers should separate Barred Warbler.

Lesser Whitethroat

Sylvia curruca (Linnaeus)

PLATE 27

FH. Fauvette babillarde   DU. Braemshuiper   IT. Bigiarella
GR. Klappersgrasmücke   SW. Ärtsångare   SP. Curruca zarcerilla

Breeding
Present in
summer only
Occurs regularly
on spring and
autumn migration

DISTRIBUTION
AND HABITAT

Eurasia from Arctic Circle southwards, throughout Europe, except for S. France and Iberian peninsula and eastward through Iran and Russian Turkestan to Manchuria and N. China. Winters in N.E. Africa, S. Iran, and N.W. India.

Generally open habitat with scrub and hedgerow, similar to that of Whitethroat, but also in more open woodland and parks, areas with taller bushes and young conifer plantations.

DESCRIPTION

Length 5¼ in (13.5 cm)

Dark, slate-grey head contrasts with brownish-grey mantle. Lores and ear coverts very dark brown and contrasting very noticeably with crown. Faint greyish-white eyestripe. Underparts whitish, occasionally with very pale pinkish flush on breast. Wings dark brown

93

with paler fringes and tail dark grey-brown, sometimes contrasting with paler grey uppertail coverts. White on outer tail feathers is barely noticeable.

Autumn immature is browner than adult, darker on crown and more olive-buff on breast and flanks.

Bill is slaty-black with a paler grey base to lower mandible. Legs are dark lead colour and iris a pale brownish-grey.

IN THE FIELD

Dark patch on ear coverts is more pronounced and noticeable than on any other white-throated European warbler. Strong similarity to Whitethroat (see below). Generally appears to have a greyish head and rump, white bordered outer tail feathers and dark ear coverts. In flight wings are broad and short. Against a dark hedge background, will usually look very grey.

SONG

Call note is a hard, persistent 'tack-tack'. Also a 'sharr-rr', similar to a Whitethroat, but emitted less frequently, and a thin, wheezy 'zit'. The song is usually delivered from deep inside a bush. It consists of a series of soft, low warbling notes to begin with, sometimes nearly inaudible, followed by a much louder, clearer, Turdine-like rattling, being a rapid repetition (seven or eight times) of a single note. This has been transcribed as 'checka-checka-checka'. The vertical song flight of the Whitethroat is lacking. Subsong is very similar to Whitethroat's.

SIMILAR
SPECIES

Most easily confused with Whitethroat, but is smaller, more compact, with a shorter tail, much greyer upperparts and no chestnut patch on the wings. More secretive in behaviour than Whitethroat. In certain locations, Lesser Whitethroat may be confused with other *Sylvia* warblers. Dark ear coverts can give a hooded appearance, but this is less apparent than in Sardinian or Rüppell's Warblers. The breast is white, not pinkish as in the Spectacled Warbler and the legs are darker bluish-grey.

For differences and similarities between Lesser Whitethroat and other *Sylvia* warblers, females and immatures, see chart on page 74.

Common Whitethroat

PLATE 27

Sylvia communis Latham

FH. Fauvette grisette   DU. Grasmus   IT. Sterpazzola
GR. Dorngrasmücke   SW. Törnsångare   SP. Curruca Zarcera

Breeding
Present in
summer only
Occurs regularly
on spring and
autumn migration

DISTRIBUTION
AND HABITAT

Europe from 64°N in Scandinavia and Russia south to Mediterranean region including N.W. Africa, eastwards across Siberia to the River Yenisei, across Russian Turkestan to N. Mongolia and W. Sinkiang and across Turkey to Iran. Migrates south and southwestwards to winter in tropical and southern Africa.

Favours fairly open localities of scrub, untrimmed hedgerows and edges of fields, thickets with tangled vegetation, and bushes. Gorse commons, osier beds, gardens. In winter in open thorn-bush, scrub, and forest edges.

DESCRIPTION

Length 5½ in (14 cm)

Upperparts of male dull brown, more tawny on rump and uppertail coverts. Crown and nape slate-grey. Whitish eye ring, brown ear coverts. Underparts

95

whitish, very noticeably the throat, contrasting with the buffish pink breast and deeper buff flanks. Undertail coverts are buff with white tips. Wings are dark brown with feathers narrowly fringed rufous. Wing coverts more broadly fringed rufous brown, giving the wing a conspicuously rusty appearance. Tail dark brown with outer side of outermost feathers greyish-white. Female has brown crown, less pink on breast and flanks, and dirtier white on outer tail feathers. A complete moult takes place after breeding so that birds on autumn migration look to be in fresh plumage.

Juveniles have darker upperparts, yellower wing coverts, and a less white throat.

Bill greyish-brown, base of lower mandible bluish-pink. Legs pale brown. Iris yellowish-brown to olive, often with a pale ring.

A cline of decreasing colour saturation and increasing size runs across the range from west to east. Numerous subspecies have been named at various points in this cline, but apart from the nominate race described above, we should note the two main subspecies: *S. c. icterops* of the E. Mediterranean, eastwards through N. Iran into Asia, which is greyer above than the main European race, less brown generally and paler on flanks and underparts. The edges of the upper wing coverts become sandy rufous. *S. c. volgensis* of E. Russia is paler again and larger than *S. c. communis*, but not as grey as *S. c. icterops*.

IN THE FIELD

A perky restless bird, spending most of its time in hedges and dense, low vegetation, from which it will suddenly emerge, then quickly disappear again with crest raised, white throat puffed out and tail spread. Then comes a harsh scolding from within the cover. Flight over any distance is undulating and the long wings and tail show up well in flight. The conspicuously rusty wings and whitish outer tail feathers, together with grey cap extending below the eye, are good field marks.

SONG

Calls are a repeated 'check', a raucous scolding 'churr' which rises in pitch slightly, or a hiss. There are two phases to the song, firstly a quiet, uniform, rapid chatter, somewhat similar to a Blackcap's warble, and then a shrill, hoarse chatter. The song is higher than a Blackcap's or a Garden Warbler's but much less musical. Males most frequently sing in bushes, moving incessantly. The courtship flight and song starts from the top of a bush and makes a tour of several vantage points before returning to the starting point, when the bird immediately vanishes again. The subsong is often heard in late summer and is much more melodious than the full song.

SIMILAR
SPECIES

In size, Whitethroat is slightly larger than Lesser Whitethroat or Blackcap, but not as large as Garden Warbler or Barred Warbler.

Compared to Garden Warbler, Whitethroat is slenderer and tail is longer. Visually quite different in coloration, particularly of underparts.

Compared to Lesser Whitethroat, Whitethroat again has a longer tail and shows rusty brown on the wings. Whitethroat is less grey in general appearance and does not have conspicuous dark grey ear coverts of Lesser Whitethroat. For indication of differences and similarities between Whitethroat and other *Sylvia* warblers see chart on page 74.

Garden Warbler

PLATE 10

Sylvia borin (Boddaert)

FH. Fauvette des jardins   DU. Tuinfluiter   IT. Beccafico
GR. Gartengrasmücke   SW. Trädgårdssångare
SP. Curraca mosquitera

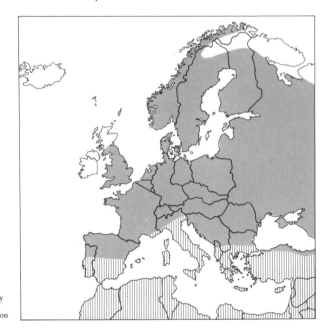

Breeding
Present in
summer only
Occurs regularly
on spring and
autumn migration

DISTRIBUTION
AND HABITAT

Europe from 70°N, Archangel and Upper Pechora basin
south to the Iberian peninsula, Italy, S.E. Europe,
Transcaucasia and western Siberia east to the River
Yenisei. Migrates to central and southern Africa, occasionally overwintering in W. Europe, including Britain.

Open deciduous or mixed woodland with plentiful
undergrowth of bushes, brambles, etc., but, unlike
Blackcap, will occupy bushy areas where no trees are
present. Occasionally in coniferous woods with deciduous secondary growth. Also hedgerows, parks and
gardens. In winter occurs in gardens, thornbush savan-
na and forest edges.

DESCRIPTION

Length 5½ in (14 cm)

Uniform brownish-olive upperparts. Lores and faint, inconspicuous supercilium pale buffish-grey. Ear coverts pale tan. Underparts whitish washed with buff, most clearly on upper breast and flanks. Undertail coverts pale brown. Wings dark brown with olive fringes to feathers. Square-ended tail is olive-brown with pale edges to outermost feathers.

Immatures may have a greenish tinge to the upperparts.

Bill dark brown, base of lower mandible yellowish. Legs greyish-brown, iris dark brown with a faint, pale eye ring.

IN THE FIELD

A plump, uniformly brown warbler with pale buffy underparts. Characteristic round head, stubby bill, and short square tail. Large eye and rather blank look is characteristic, but lack of obvious distinguishing features is probably first clue to identity. Greyish legs can be a good separating mark from *Phylloscopus* warblers.

SONG

The usual hard *Sylvia* 'tack-tack' call note, and a low, grating 'churr'. Also, most frequently heard in autumn, a plaintive 'whit'. Alarm call is a series of agitated, high, harsh scolding notes. The song is a smooth, even warble, somewhat similar to Blackcap's but quieter, lower-pitched, and sustained much longer. Generally sings whilst hidden in undergrowth. Like Orphean Warbler, song can recall a thrush due to lack of harsh notes. Clarity of notes is usually remarked upon, but Garden Warbler usually omits the high notes of the Blackcap's song.

SIMILAR SPECIES

Lack of distinctive characteristics, whilst giving a clue to this bird's identity, can cause great confusion with other species. It can resemble smaller, unstreaked *Acrocephalus* warblers, but they have long, rounded tails, and usually longer bills.

Hippolais warblers may also be confused but, except for Booted which is much smaller, they all have longer bills and different headshapes. Care is nevertheless needed in ruling out *Hippolais*.

Grey-brown legs of Garden Warbler help to distinguish it from Olivaceous, Booted, or immature Barred Warbler.

Blackcap should not be confused if crown is seen well, but if not, short tail of Garden Warbler will help and difference in habitat is usually marked.

Leg colour will also help to distinguish Garden Warbler from Chiffchaff and Willow Warbler, but both are noticeably smaller.

Blackcap

PLATE 25

Sylvia atricapilla (Linnaeus)

FH. Fauvette à tête noire   DU. Zwartkop
IT. Capinera   GR. Mönchsgrasmücke
SW. Svarthätta   SP. Curraca capirotada

Breeding
Present in
summer only
Occurs regularly
on spring and
autumn migration
Breeding
Present through-
out the year
Occurs in
winter

DISTRIBUTION
AND HABITAT

Europe east to W. Siberia, south to the Mediterranean and N.W. Africa. Middle East and Caucasus eastward to S. Caspian region in Iran. Also Canary Is., Madeira, Azores, and Cape Verde Is. Migrates to S. Europe and Africa from the Mediterranean south to Upper Guinea in the west and Tanzania in the east. Some winter in W. Europe as far north as Britain and Ireland.

Mature woodland with bramble undergrowth and thick shrub layer. Also overgrown hedges, fruit bushes, scrub with scattered trees, gardens, and parks. In C. Europe also in conifer woods. In winter in evergreen forest and thick undergrowth.

DESCRIPTION

Length 5½ in (14 cm)
   Upperparts of adult male are brownish-olive

becoming greyer on the nape and rump. Crown is jet-black and wings and tail dark brown without any white. Underparts are dirty white washed with olive on the breast and flanks. The female adult is browner on upperparts and a clear rufous on the crown where the male is black. Female underparts are buffier than male's. In both male and female the crown colour does not extend below eye.

Immatures are more rufous above and yellower below. First winter males usually have a mixture of black and brown on the crowns, and some males in immature plumage have crowns exactly like adult females.

Bill is slaty black, paler and greyer below. Legs dark slate. Iris brown; eye ring whitish.

Coloration in Europe is clinal with populations becoming paler and slightly larger as they range to the east. The two main races are *S. a. atricapilla* in the north and west, and *S. a. dammholzi* in the south and east. Some differentiation is also evident in the isolated Mediterranean island populations.

IN THE FIELD

Very active and lively and less retiring than many warblers, but often stays well hidden. Flight is swift and jerky and the long wings and tail are clearly noticeable. The male is a greyish-looking bird, the female less so, but once the crowns are observed there is no doubt of their identity.

SONG

A variety of call notes, including a hard, scolding 'tack-tack', rapidly repeated when excited, a 'churr' similar to Garden Warbler, a creaky 'swerr', and a somewhat plaintive 'pheu'. The song has a stumbling start, but then becomes rich and melodious, and may be confused with a Garden Warbler's but Blackcap's has more rhythmic and definite form and phrasing, and is higher pitched and more sustained. It is often louder towards the end, where there is frequently a flute-like flourish. Male Blackcaps usually sing hidden deep in foliage. The song may recall a thin, high-pitched Blackbird, the tempo being extremely similar.

SIMILAR SPECIES

Sardinian and Orphean Warblers both have black caps, but both have more black than male Blackcap and both have conspicuous white in the tail. In all other black-capped warblers, the black crown terminates below the eye. Song may be confused with that of Garden Warbler (see above) but rhythmical phrasing of Blackcap's song is soon recognizable. Some call notes are also very similar to Garden Warblers', so a sighting is generally required to ensure correct identification.

Phylloscopus

Known as Leaf Warblers or Willow Warblers; they should be referred to generically as the former to prevent confusion with the species *Phylloscopus trochilus*, commonly called the Willow Warbler. The genus consists of about 34 species which are in general alpine or subalpine in habitat, and the mountain ranges of the Himalayan region show the greatest variety of forms. In Europe where the extent of mountain habitat is much poorer and less diverse, there are correspondingly fewer species, and these include three which are in the process of colonizing Europe from Asia. In addition to the alpine forms there exist two or three tropical forms which do not concern us in this regional guide.

In form, Leaf Warblers are small slender birds. They have tails with 12 feathers, the sexes are alike, and the juveniles are dull editions of the adults. In coloration there are broadly two types; the more usual is some shade of green or olive-green above and yellowish below, while the minority have brownish upper parts and whitish, or buff and white underparts. Some species may be exclusively one or the other, and some may show a clinal change from one extreme to the other across their distributional ranges.

They are active and restless birds, constantly searching the foliage for food, and flying out to take insects. They are normally found in trees, from the lower branches up to the canopy, or in bushes adjacent to woods. They are not gregarious but some may loosely associate with other birds in feeding parties. The flight is jerky and flitting and does not seem capable of being sustained for long journeys. They are both sedentary, and in the case of birds breeding in the northern Palaearctic, strongly migratory.

On the basis of identifiable plumage characteristics, Williamson (1962) has divided the genus into sections which may be helpful in distinguishing species. The first division may be made broadly geographically between

Asiatic species which winter from India eastwards, and European species with winter quarters largely in Africa. Williamson's subdivisions then may be applied as follows:

1. ASIATIC LEAF WARBLERS

(a) Yellow-rumped species and their allies. Very small size. Main characteristics of plumage are a well-defined supercilium, a distinct double wing bar, dark coronal bands separated by a mesial stripe along the centre of the crown, tertials with pale outer edges and tips, a yellow rump band and white on the three outermost tail feathers. *Phylloscopus pulcher, maculipennis, proregulus, subviridis, inornatus.*

(b) Crowned species and their allies. Medium to small size. Strongly marked supercilium, a double wing bar (except in one case), well-defined coronal bands and pale mesial stripe and some white in outer tail feathers. This group do not have a yellow rump band nor pale edges and tips to tertials. *Phylloscopus occipitalis, coronatus, reguloides, cantator, davisoni, ricketti.*

(c) Arctic and Greenish Warblers and their allies. Medium to large size. Well-defined supercilium, double wing bar (but upper bar may be very faint). They do not have coronal bands or mesial stripe, but crown is usually darker than mantle. Very little white on tail feathers, no yellow band on rump and no pale edges and tips to tertials. *Phylloscopus borealis, trochiloides, nitidus, plumbeitarsus, tenellipes, magnirostris, tytleri.*

(d) Remaining Asiatic species. These are mainly ground feeders, as opposed to arboreal preference of the rest. Well-marked supercilium, but none of the clear plumage characteristics of the other Asiatic species. Large to medium size. *Phylloscopus fuscatus, fuligiventer, schwarzi, griseolus, armandii, affinis* (including *subaffinis*).

2. MAINLY EUROPEAN LEAF WARBLERS

These lack all the plumage characteristics exhibited by Asiatic groups, except for a faint to moderate supercilium, and in one case (*P. bonelli*) some yellow on the rump. They include both the yellow-greenish and the brown-whitish varieties, and are small to large in size.

Phylloscopus trochilus, collybita, sibilatrix, bonelli, and two fringe species *neglectus* and *sindianus.*

In Europe there are six breeding species, two being on the fringe of our area. This guide covers another five which occur as regular to accidental visitors to Europe, mainly in the late autumn migration.

Green Warbler

PLATE 3

Phylloscopus nitidus (Blyth)

FH. Pouillot vert   IT. Lui nitido
GR. Kaukasus Grunlaubsänger   SP. Mosquitero verde

Breeding
Present in
summer only

DISTRIBUTION
AND HABITAT

Caucasus from Black Sea to northern Iran and Afghanistan. Migrates south through Pakistan to southern India and Sri Lanka, and back via Himalayan foothills and eastern India before turning west to breeding area. Mountainous areas with woods with thick undergrowth. Beech or juniper bushes preferred. In winter in more general woodland as well as parks, gardens, orchards or other cultivation.

DESCRIPTION

Length 4¼ in (11 cm)
    Bright greenish upperparts and all yellow underparts. Bright yellow cheeks and supercilium and pale yellow wing bar. In fresh plumage, second narrow wing bar may be visible.
    First winter birds are similar to adults after autumn

107

body moult, but adults will have wing and tail feathers very abraded and wing bar much reduced.

Bill is dark brown above with a whitish tip and a white line along the cutting edges. Lower mandible is creamy at base, brownish in centre, and whitish at tip. Legs deep olive to dark grey.

IN THE FIELD Keeps well hidden in undergrowth, but active and restless. Mostly in trees. Combination of bright green and yellow with strongly defined supercilium should make identification easy, but in certain poor light in thick cover it may look remarkably colourless.

SONG Call note is a cheerful 'chi-wee', or sometimes a triple note, transcribed as 'thir-irr-ip', very similar in tone to Greenish Warbler (of which Green Warbler was considered a race by many authorities). Song is a repetitive 'tiss-tri-tiss' uttered over and over again. The song has been said to be similar to that of the Willow Warbler, but Green's is far less musical or expressive and much more monotonous.

SIMILAR SPECIES Like a small, brightly coloured Wood Warbler, but is brighter Green above and all yellow below, instead of white belly of Wood Warbler. General tone of yellow is softer than that of Wood Warbler.

Greenish Warbler has less yellow but more sharply marked supercilium, and conversely, Green's wing bar is more pronounced than that of Greenish.

Greenish Warbler

PLATE 28

Phylloscopus trochiloides (Sundevall)

FH. Pouillot terne (verdâtre)   DU. Grauwe fitis
IT. Lui verdastro   GR. Grüner Laubsänger
SW. Lundsångare   SP. Mosquitero troquiloide

Breeding
Present in
summer only

DISTRIBUTION
AND HABITAT

From Baltic coast and southern Finland east to Sea of Okhotsk and western China. Migrates to India and northern Indochina. Recent expansion of range into N.W. Europe since turn of this century but has increased more rapidly in last 30 years, with a growing number of occurrences in Britain. May be found from sea-level to 11 000 ft, but in the north of the range usually breeds near sea-level. Favours forest edges and open woodland, but on migration and in winter in undergrowth and bushes in both deciduous and coniferous woodland.

DESCRIPTION

Length 4¼ in (11 cm)
    Greenish-grey upperparts, becoming greyer towards autumn. Head slightly darker than mantle. Well-

marked pale yellow supercilium contrasts strongly with dark eyestreak. Underparts dirty white with greyish flanks. Undertail coverts yellowish-white. Wings and tail brown, wings with narrow white bar. Tail has dirty white outer webs. First-winter birds are brighter than adults. Adults, in autumn, have tail and wing feathers much worn and wing bar may become very indistinct. Bill is dark brown above and light yellowish-brown below, sometimes slightly orange at base. Legs dark greyish-brown, occasionally lighter. Mouth yellow.

IN THE FIELD Like small, short-tailed and very smart Willow Warbler. Extremely active, greenish above and whitish below with distinctive long supercilium, and single white wingbar. Constantly moving through foliage picking insects off leaves and occasionally fluttering at branch-ends. Usually keeps well hidden despite activity, and is normally located by call. Head and nape look greyest part of plumage. Continual restless tail flicking and may hold wings loosely closed, the tips drooping below the level of back and tail.

SONG Call note is a monosyllabic high-pitched whistle, 'psi' or may be doubled occasionally. Also a quieter 'see-see', almost disyllabic. The song is of short duration, commencing with a loud rapidly repeated call note merging into a Wren-like gabble. The song lasts only two or three seconds, then may be repeated after a pause of five to seven seconds. It is rapid, resonant and very high pitched, transcribed as 'ti-psi-tyu, psi-tyu, psi-ti-ti-ti-ti, psi . . .'. It is usually delivered from within tree canopy and may be heard on both spring and autumn passage. There may also be a short, curious humming sound, sometimes attached to the song, sometimes quite isolated.

SIMILAR SPECIES May be confused with several other *Phylloscopus* Warblers, being particularly similar to eastern races of the Chiffchaff, but wing bar is clearer and supercilium much broader, clearer, and longer.
Arctic Warbler is larger and has an even more conspicuous supercilium and wing bar. Arctic's legs are paler.
Yellow-browed Warbler is smaller, but again has a more conspicuous supercilium, two wing bars and

greyish-brown legs, not as pale as Arctic's. Chiffchaff and Willow Warbler are generally duller in plumage, both lacking wing bar and clear supercilium, but additionally both have yellow underwing coverts, compared to white of Greenish Warbler.

Arctic Warbler

PLATE 28

Phylloscopus borealis (Blasius)

FH. Pouillot boréal   DU. Noordse boszanger
IT. Lui boreale   GR. Nordischer Laubsänger
SW. Nordsångare   SP. Mosquitero boreal

Breeding
Present in
summer only

DISTRIBUTION AND HABITAT

Northern Scandinavia east to Bering Strait and north to limit of forest. South to 68°N in Russia. Migrates through eastern China, Japan, and Indochina to winter in S.E. Asia, Indonesia, and Philippine Is. Vagrant almost annually to western Europe and Britain. Birds breeding in northern Scandinavia move eastwards on migration into Siberia before turning south towards China.

In damp conifer or mixed forest, especially birch and pine not far from water. Also swampy woods and willow scrub. On passage also in tall grass and bushes.

DESCRIPTION

Length 4¾ in (12 cm)

Upperparts and edges to tail and wing feathers olive with grey-brown tinge. Darker on crown and brighter olive on rump. Conspicuous, yellow-white supercilium reaching almost to the hindcrown and appearing to be upcurved at the rear. Supercilium edged below with distinct dark line. Underparts dull, creamy white varied with a few yellow streaks. Sides of breast and flanks shaded brownish-olive. Undertail coverts buffy yellow. Wings and tail dark brown. Two wing bars in fresh plumage, the upper one white and the lower yellow, but these get abraded by mid-year. Tips of tail feathers whitish. After body moult in autumn, upperparts become a purer greenish-olive. First-winter birds are darker greenish-olive above and yellower below than adults. Autumn adults have wings and tail faded pale brown and may have lost one or both wing bars.

Bill dark brown above, orange-yellow below (first-winter birds pale brown below). Mouth orange. Legs pale brown.

IN THE FIELD

A large and active, but typical *Phylloscopus*, hopping and flitting about the canopy, sometimes hovering and making small sallies from tree tops. Occasionally in lower vegetation. Best distinguished by very long up-turned supercilium, pale dagger-like bill and very pale legs, pale throat, call, and restless behaviour with much tail and wing flicking. Said to prefer walls and fences on migration.

SONG

Call note is a long, loud, and piercing 'tswee-ep' or a hard 'zik' or 'chit'. Sometimes heard to give a scolding chatter not unlike a Lesser Whitethroat or a soft Mistle Thrush (*Turdus viscivorus*). Also a double call, reminiscent of a wagtail—'hissick'.

Song is a resonant and powerful, buzzing 'tzi-tzi-tzi-tzi' followed by a rapid trill. Whole song lasts only about two seconds. A shy singer and is most reliably identified by song. This may remind the listener of a distant Chaffinch (*F. coelebs*) before that bird's song begins its characteristic descent.

SIMILAR SPECIES

Larger and slimmer than Willow Warbler with wing-bar, supercilium, and whiter underparts. Greenish Warbler is most likely to be confused, but this has dark legs compared to Arctic's pale ones. Wood Warbler has no white throat and much shorter and less distinct supercilium.

Pallas' Leaf Warbler

PLATE 29

Phylloscopus proregulus (Pallas)

FH. Pouillot de Pallas   DU. Pallas' boszanger
IT. Lui del Pallas   GR. Goldhähnchenlaubsänger
SW. Kungsfågelsångare   SP. Mosquitero de Pallas

DISTRIBUTION
AND HABITAT

Russian Altai Mts. eastwards to Sakhalin I., N. Mongolia, C. China, and west to Himalayas. Migrates to S. China, N.E. India, and Indochina. Occurring in W. Europe with increasing frequency.

Coniferous and mixed woods, but also bushes and scrub. Birches and pine forests in breeding season, but in lighter growth in winter such as scrub along river beds or forest glades and edges.

DESCRIPTION

Length 3½ in (9 cm)

Upperparts and edges to tail and wing feathers uniform bright olive-green. Pale crown stripe with indistinct dark olive coronal bands on either side of it. Lemon-yellow band across rump. Clearly marked superciliary, yellow in front of eye and whiter behind eye, but meeting at base of upper mandible to form a yellow forehead. Eyestreak dark olive, cheeks golden, and ear coverts pale olive and yellow. Underparts dull white turning yellowish on flanks. Undertail coverts pale yellow. Wings and tail brown with two prominent yellow wing bars, the lower being particularly wide and clear.

Bill dark brown, base of lower mandible pale yellow. Mouth yellow. Legs dark brown.

IN THE FIELD

Smallest leaf warbler in Europe. Habits are similar to Goldcrest, notably fluttering outside foliage cover to pick insects off outer leaves. Yellow rump band is very visible during this action. May also launch further out from foliage in short flycatching sallies. Striped crown is most noticeable when seen from behind. May often be seen in parties with tits and Goldcrests, but is seldom seen to hang upside down.

Best field marks are small size, wingbars, yellow rump, and crown pattern.

SONG

Call note is a high-pitched, shrill 'swee' or 'seep', less squeaky and more prolonged than Goldcrest. Also a more metallic 'choot', and a double 'choo-ee' with the second syllable higher than the first. Song is strongly uttered and consists of various melodious notes repeated four or five times. The notes may be a short series of variations on the single call note, or several very similar notes together in a phrase which is then repeated.

SIMILAR
SPECIES

Yellow-browed Warbler—slightly larger, no crown stripe, less yellow on rump, duller olive-green upper-parts. Also call note slurred into one syllable.

Goldcrest and Firecrest—no yellow on rump, more black on the head. Call is squeakier and slightly higher-pitched.

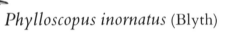

Yellow-browed Warbler PLATE 29

Phylloscopus inornatus (Blyth)

FH. Pouillot à grande sourcils   DU. Bladkoninkje
IT. Lui forestiero   GR. Gelbbrauenlaubsänger
SW. Vitbrynad sångare   SP. Mosquitero bilistado

DISTRIBUTION
AND HABITAT

Asia from northern Ural Mts. to Sea of Okhotsk and Ussuri River, and through Russian and Chinese Turkestan to W. Himalayas. Migrates to S. China, India, Afghanistan, Indochina, and Malaysia. Accidental to N.W. Europe, but regularly recorded in autumn in Britain.

Prefers gardens and mixed woodland to dense evergreen forests. Often in willows. In winter may be found in any scrub or undergrowth.

DESCRIPTION

Length 4 in (10 cm)

Upperparts and fringes of wing and tail feathers bright olive-green. Rump lighter and head darker. Broad yellowish supercilium almost to nape contrasting sharply with dark streak through eye. Occasionally, a pale stripe along centre of crown. Underparts generally white with varying amounts and tones of yellow. Yellowish-white undertail coverts. Wings and tail dark brown. Conspicuous double yellowish-white wing bars. During summer the upperparts are abraded to a greyish-brown, but rump retains its greenish tinge and supercilium goes white, except for rear part. There are reports of adults with plumage so worn that upper wingbars are abraded completely. Juveniles have more buff on head and underparts.

Bill brown with base of lower mandible yellowish and tip dark horn. Legs grey-brown. Mouth yellowish.

IN THE FIELD

Pale greenish-yellow appearance, smaller than Willow Warbler, with pale yellow supercilium. Off-white underparts, double wing bar, and greenish rump. Often in parties with other *Phylloscopi* and Tits (*Parus* spp). Tail looks disproportionately short and appears to have no white in it. Keeps high up in trees except in high winds and usually stays lower down on migration and in winter. Look for grey-brown legs. Occasionally flutters against the bark of a tree or to the ground.

SONG

Call note is a loud 'weest' or 'tiss-yip' high-pitched and sharper than Willow Warbler's call. Song is short and weak, a few plaintive notes similar to the call note, but ending in a peculiar buzzing noise, the whole being transcribed as 'tss, tss, tss, tss, tsit, zhzhii'.

SIMILAR
SPECIES

May be confused with Pallas' Warbler when Yellow-browed has crown streak, but Pallas' dark brown and yellow head pattern is distinctive. Separated from juvenile Goldcrest by larger size and conspicuous supercilium. Song has been likened to twittering of Siskin (*Carduelis spinus*) but call is louder and more clearly disyllabic than either Chiffchaff or Willow Warbler. Lack of yellow on rump distinguishes Yellow-browed from other Asian *Phylloscopi*, *P. pulcher* (Orange-barred Leaf Warbler) and *P. maculipennis* (Ashy-throated Leaf Warbler).

Radde's Warbler

PLATE 12

Phylloscopus schwarzi (Radde)

FH. Pouillot de Schwarz   IT. Lui di Radde
GR. Bartlaubsänger   SP. Mosquitero de Schwarz

DISTRIBUTION AND HABITAT

Siberia and Russian Altai east to Sakhalin Is. Migrates through central and eastern China to winter in Indochina. Vagrant to Europe and accidental in Britain.

Clearings and edges of pine forests. In winter in bushes and tall trees. Particularly favours rhododendrons, but keeps well concealed and close to the ground.

DESCRIPTION

Length 5 in (12.5 cm)

Upperparts brownish-olive, browner on head and becoming greenish on rump. Broad conspicuous supercilium from base of bill to hind crown, buff as far as ear coverts, whitish beyond. Eye line and line above supercilium contrasting blackish brown. Cheeks buff mottled with brown. Chin and throat white. There is a variously distinct buffish pectoral band above a dull white belly, occasionally streaked yellow. Undertail coverts buffish-brown with yellow-orange tinge. Wings and tail olive-brown, outermost tail feathers tipped whitish. Tail noticeably long. In autumn upperparts more greenish-olive, head browner, and rump greener. Whole underparts washed with buff brown streaked with yellow, palest in centre of belly.

Bill noticeably stout and broad, blackish above and orange-horn below with dusky tip. Legs strong and straw yellow. Mouth bright chrome yellow.

IN THE FIELD

Larger, bulkier, and longer-tailed than Chiffchaff. Long creamy supercilium and blackish eyestreak are distinctive, combined with plain brownish upperparts and pale underparts. Pale, strong, yellowish legs are important identification feature. Very skulking, usually in low cover. When seen, may be perching in upright stance like a Reed Warbler.

SONG

Call is a soft, whistling 'tsit' or 'quit', nervous and anxious in tone, and frequently repeated. Song is a loud and beautiful series of trills, each starting with two or three introductory notes. Successive trills are of differing pitch and tone and the whole is reminiscent of a Nightingale (*L. megarhynchos*) without its single notes. Alarm note is a soft twitter without harsh or staccato notes.

For similarities and differences between Radde's and Dusky Warbler, see under Dusky Warbler (p. 121). Size and shape may confuse with Arctic Warbler which also has broad conspicuous supercilium, but which also has a distinctive wing bar. There may be possible confusion with Milne-Edwards' Leaf Warbler (*Phylloscopus armandii*), both having yellow in underparts, but *armandii* is definitely streaked, as opposed to more uniform colour of Radde's. Confusion may also arise initially with Garden Warbler as both species generally lack strong plumage features, except for Radde's supercilium. There is a noticeable difference in bill size.

Dusky Warbler

PLATE 3

Phylloscopus fuscatus (Blyth)

FH. Pouillot brun   IT. Lui scuro   GR. Dunkler Laubsänger
SP. Mosquitero sombrio

DISTRIBUTION
AND HABITAT

River Ob eastward to Sea of Okhotsk, south to the Altai Mts., Mongolia, Manchuria, Sakhalin, and western China to eastern Himalayas. Migrates to southern China, Indochina, eastern and northern India. Accidental in Europe.

Not arboreal and avoids wooded country. Prefers low scrub and bushes in mountainous country in humid or arid open regions. Frequently found in marshy areas. On migration may be found in hedges and standing crops in damp areas.

DESCRIPTION

Length 4¼ in (11 cm)

Upperparts, tail, and wings dusky olive-brown. Very distinct supercilium, whitish in front, rusty white over and behind eye. Pale semi-eye ring. Eyestreak dark brown, cheeks and ear coverts rusty. Throat white, breast and belly creamier white with grey on sides. Flanks rusty, undertail coverts and inner edges to secondaries fulvous-white. No wingbars. Sexes alike. First-winter birds show some yellow in centre of belly and an olive tinge to upperparts.

Bill, upper mandible, and tip of lower dark brown; remainder yellow. Legs reddish-brown in front, paler and greener behind. Mouth yellow.

IN THE FIELD

Looks like a warm-coloured Reed Warbler with a very prominent supercilium, but is not reddish enough either above or below. Affects a horizontal carriage, but the flattish head and fluttering wing action are typically phylloscopine. Has the darkest plumage of any European *Phylloscopus* and lacks any green or yellow coloration. Always a skulker but may often feed on the ground. Flicks wings and tail repeatedly.

SONG

Call note is a *Sylvia*-like 'tack' or a hard, low, clicking note, frequently repeated. Song is reported to be monotonous but strong and musical 'tia, tia, tia, tiaaa', followed by a trill said to resemble the subdued stridulation of a Magpie (*Pica pica*).

SIMILAR
SPECIES

Except for Radde's Warbler, Dusky is distinguished from all other *Phylloscopi* without wingbars by heavy whitish supercilium. This feature also separates Radde's and Dusky from unstreaked *Acrocephalus* Warblers. An excellent review of the similarities and differences between Radde's and Dusky has been given by Williamson (1974) and some of his comments are summarized here.

	Dusky Warbler	Radde's Warbler
Upperparts	Uniform brown tinged with rufous. Looks greyer in autumn	Olive-brown in spring, greenish-olive in autumn, especially on rump
Head pattern	Supercilium dull rusty white to end of ear coverts. Rusty cheeks. Eyes appear normal size	Supercilium long, broad, creamy extending to nape. Thin blackish eyebrow above and stripe through eye. Eyes look abnormally large
Underparts	Dull and uniform greyish white, including flanks and undertail coverts	White throat, yellowish breast and belly. Flanks buff. Undertail coverts orangy-buff.
Bill	Typical fine, short *Phylloscopus* bill	Noticeably long and broad
Legs	Reddish brown, slender	Thick, strong, pale straw coloured
General style and movements	Similar to Chiffchaff, but flicks wings and spreads tail constantly. A skulker that feeds close to the ground on migration	Looks bulky and heavy. Movements deliberate. Noticeably long tail. A skulker that feeds close to the ground on migration
Calls	Loud 'chek' or 'chak'. Definite and confident. Infrequently repeated more than twice. Staccato, chattering alarm	Clipped 'quit' or 'twit'. Frequently repeated. Conveys nervous anxiety. Alarm softer and less harsh and staccato

Bonelli's Warbler

PLATE 30

Phylloscopus bonelli (Vieillot)

FH. Pouillot de Bonelli   DU. Bergfluiter
IT. Lui bianco   GR. Berglaubsänger
SW. Bergsångare   SP. Mosquitero papialbo

Breeding
Present in summer only
Occurs regularly on spring and autumn migration

DISTRIBUTION
AND HABITAT

Northwest Africa and continental Europe north to S. Germany and Czechoslovakia, east to Bulgaria, Greece, Turkey, and Israel. Migrates through the Sahara to winter in West Africa, and through the eastern Mediterranean to the Sudan. Vagrant to Britain. The race in W. Europe and N. Africa, as far east as Italy is *P. b. bonelli*, whereas east from Yugoslavia it is *P. b. orientalis*.

Found normally in hills and mountains from 2000 ft to 6000 ft. Chiefly in oak or pine forests in dense foliage, but also in open cork-oak groves and areas of sparse, dry, scrub vegetation.

DESCRIPTION

Length 4½ in (11 cm)

Upperparts greyish-brown, often with close greenish-yellow streaks. Rump and edges of tail and wing feathers bright greenish-yellow to golden brown, contrasting with mantle. Supercilium whitish, turning to yellow above the eye and dying away altogether in front of the eye. Underparts silky white with grey at flanks and sides of breast. Wings and tail dark brown with no wingbar. Underwing coverts yellowish. Outer and penultimate tail feathers have very narrow white border, usually difficult to see. First-winter birds have greyer mantles than adults and contrast between mantle and rump not nearly so pronounced.

Bill, horn coloured above and pinkish below. Mouth yellow. Legs brown with pinkish tinge behind. Eastern race is distinctly greyer on upperparts than nominate.

IN THE FIELD   Active and agile, but unobtrusive and generally keeps well hidden. General impression is of a bird with a very pale, colourless front half and a darker more colour-marked rear half. Rump colour is difficult to see in the field and easier characteristics to notice are greyness of head, whiteness of underparts, supercilium and yellowish wing patches where fringes of inner primaries and secondaries overlap.

SONG   Call of 'hoo-eet' is less plaintive than Willow Warbler and more obviously disyllabic, metallic in tone. Song is a loose trill on the same note, slower, more musical and more clearly separated than that of Wood Warbler. It does not accelerate like Wood Warbler's song.

SIMILAR
SPECIES   Chiffchaff—much less grey on uppersides and without yellowish rump or wing patches.

Willow Warbler—some yellow on underparts compared to none at all on Bonelli's. Supercilium clearer in front of eye. Calls need careful separation.

Wood Warbler—see above for song distinction, but song could also be confused with Lesser Whitethroat or a distant Cirl Bunting (*Emberiza cirlus*). Wood Warbler's yellow breast and larger size should safely separate it visually.

Wood Warbler

PLATE 30

Phylloscopus sibilatrix (Bechstein)

FH. Pouillot siffleur   DU. Fluiter
IT. Lui verde   GR. Waldlaubsänger
SW. Grönsångare   SP. Mosquitero silbador

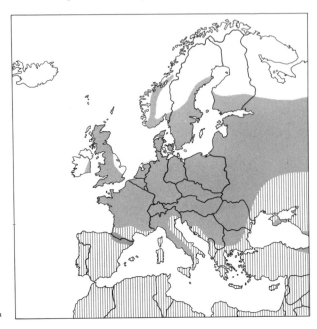

Breeding
Present in
summer only
Occurs regularly
on spring and
autumn migration

DISTRIBUTION
AND HABITAT

Most of Europe, from British Isles north to 61°N in Norway, 64°N in Sweden, Finland, and Russia, east to Ural Mts. and south to central France, Italy, Yugoslavia, Caucasus, and Crimea.

Migrates through N. Africa and eastern Mediterranean to west, central, and east Africa.

Coniferous, mixed or deciduous woodland, particularly oak and beech. Good canopy is more important than ground cover. In winter and on passage in more open, bushy country as well as in woodland.

DESCRIPTION

Length 5 in (12.5 cm)

Upperparts greenish-brown with well-marked yellowish supercilium and dark olive eyestreak. Underparts yellow on throat and upper breast, sharply demarcated from silky white belly and undertail coverts. Wings and tail dark brown with bright yellowish-green fringes.

First-winter birds are generally less vivid but edges to wing feathers are still bright yellow-green.

Bill blackish above, yellowish horn below. Legs pale yellow-brown.

IN THE FIELD   The largest leaf warbler present in Europe. Longer wings and brighter and more contrasted colour areas than other European *Phylloscopi*. Does not flick its wings, but often hangs them loosely. Actively searches for insects in the high canopy with frequent sallies and hovering. The display flight is a hovering descent whilst singing. Best field marks are greenish-yellow upperparts contrasting with yellow breast and white belly. Tail appears to be abnormally short in relation to wings and body. Rather stout, solid appearance.

SONG   Call is a mellow plaintive 'piu' very similar to a Bullfinch (*Pyrrhula pyrrhula*). Also a soft 'whit, whit, whit' like a Nuthatch (*Sitta europaea*) but less resonant. The song may be the 'piu' call note repeated many times or a high-pitched, hissed 'spi-spi-spi' followed by a trill, beginning slowly and accelerating to a long-drawn-out final note. This said to resemble the jingling of a bunch of keys and during this song the wings may be shivered. There is also a less frequently heard alternative song consisting of a monosyllabic, slow, descending 'tyoo, tyoo, tyoo', a most plaintive noise.

SIMILAR   Like a large, bright Chiffchaff with much longer wings.
SPECIES   Green Warbler has all yellow underparts and a wingbar. *Hippolais* warblers have different shaped heads and generally larger bills, but combination of yellow breast and white belly should safely isolate this bird from all other warblers.

Chiffchaff

PLATE 31

Phylloscopus collybita (Vieillot)

FH. Pouillot véloce   DU. Tjiftjaf   IT. Lui piccolo
GR. Zilpzalp   SW. Gransångare   SP. Mosquitero comun

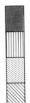

Breeding
Present in
summer only

Occurs regularly
on spring and
autumn migration

Breeding
Present through-
out the year

Occurs in
winter

DISTRIBUTION
AND HABITAT

From Scandinavia, British Isles, and Canary Islands to basin of Kolyma river. Also northwest Africa and isolated populations in Caucasia and the Himalayan region. In Europe there are two main races. In western and southern Europe is *P. c. collybita*, whilst in Scandinavia and eastern Europe is *P. c. abietinus*. In addition there are separately named races in northwest Africa (*P. c. ibericus*) and in the Canary Islands. The isolated Asian races are now considered to be a separate species, *Phylloscopus sindianus* known as the Mountain Chiffchaff.

Both *P. c. collybita* and *P. c. abietinus* migrate to north and northeast Africa, and isolated areas in west and east Africa.

Deciduous and coniferous woodlands with undergrowth, and bushes on woodland edges. Very similar habitat to that of Willow Warbler, but generally demands taller trees and fewer bushes. In the south of the range it occurs more in the mountains, and in winter more frequently found in crops and bush country than in woodland.

DESCRIPTION

Length 4¼ in (11 cm)

A cline of decreasing colour runs from north Africa to north Norway. Additionally there is a reduction of colour from west to east, but this is not an even cline as is the longitudinal one in western Europe. The nominate race in western Europe has upperparts brownisholive with slight yellow-olive tinge to the rump. Indistinct yellow-white supercilium. Underparts dirty white, streaked yellow on breast and buff on flanks. Undertail coverts yellowish white. Wings and tail brown with light yellow-olive fringes. First-winter birds are brighter and sharper in colour.

Bill dark horn, yellowish-brown at base of lower mandible. Legs very dark brown. Iris brown. Eastern and northern race is greyer above and whiter below, but is otherwise very similar.

IN THE FIELD

Usually the first migrating warbler to arrive in northern Europe. Very similar in habits to Willow Warbler, but tends to flick tail constantly when feeding. Very agile in movements, searching continually for insects. Visually the bird appears to be drably coloured, without noticeable plumage characteristics and is normally recognized by its distinctive song which starts immediately on arrival in spring and continues through to the end of July at least, though getting more sporadic at that stage.

SONG

Call is a soft 'hweet', very similar to call of Willow Warbler, but sharper and more distinctly two syllables. The song is quite unique and consists of measured repetitions of the same brief resonant syllables which give the bird its name. The same two notes are deliberately repeated in irregular order—'tsiff-tsaff-tsiff-tsiff-tsaff-tsiff-tsaff'. The song may continue for several minutes, then will recommence after only a brief pause.

SIMILAR SPECIES

The only confusing bird will be the Willow Warbler. Unless one of the two songs are heard, the species can look very similar. Chiffchaff is dingier, browner, and less yellow in colour; also more compact in shape, albeit still a small and delicate-looking bird. Chiffchaff is more buff on flanks, but supercilium is less strongly pronounced. Chiffchaff's wings are slightly shorter, the head more rounded and the legs usually darker. Leg colour is by no means a safe distinction, since Chiffchaffs occasionally have pale legs and, more often, Willow Warblers dark ones.

Compared to Bonelli's Warbler, Chiffchaff is less grey and has no yellow rump.

Compared with Greenish and Arctic Warblers, Chiffchaff has no wingbar.

Willow Warbler

Phylloscopus trochilus (Linnaeus)

FH. Pouillot fitis   DU. Fitis   IT. Lui grosso   GR. Fitis
SW. Lövsångare   SP. Mosquitero musical

Breeding
Present in
summer only
Occurs regularly
on spring and
autumn migration

DISTRIBUTION
AND HABITAT

Almost throughout northern Palaearctic from Scandinavia, British Isles, and France east across Europe and Asia
to upper Anadyr River. Winters in Portugal, east across
southern Europe and to tropical and southern Africa.

Breeds in great variety of woodland and is usually
found in broad-leaved forests or open woodland, or in
bushy and sparsely wooded areas, parks, and gardens.
On migration, in addition to these habitats, may be
found in orchards, hedgerows, willows, and ditches, in
vegetation beside open water or in reedbeds.

DESCRIPTION

Length 4¾ in (11 cm)
This bird has a dimorphic population ranging from
olive-green and yellow dominance in the southwest of
its range, to brown and white dominance in the northeast. The types of the extremes are marked by racial

names *P. t. trochilus* and *P. t. yakutensis* respectively. Between these two extremes lie varieties of intergradation. An intermediate stage is described as *P. t. acredula*, but the limits of these races are impossible to fix exactly.

The typical race in Europe has the upperparts and edges of tail and wing feathers olive-brown with a yellow-green wash. Supercilium is indistinct and yellowish in colour. Underparts dull whitish variously streaked with yellow, mostly on throat and breast. Undertail coverts yellowish-white. Wings and tail brown, without wingbars or any white in tail feathers. First-winter birds have uniform canary yellow underparts, but tinged with buff on breast. They lack adult's contrasting yellow on breast and white on belly.

Bill brown, base of lower mandible paler. Legs usually pale brown but occasionally dark brown. Iris hazel.

IN THE FIELD   The most abundant summer visitor to the northern half of Europe. A restless bird, continuously hunting through foliage for food, occasionally making little sallies from the trees to catch flying insects with acrobatic ease, or hovering to pick insects from outside leaves. Almost no visual distinguishing marks and normally identified by song, but look for leg colour, which may help to identify it during the breeding season.

SONG   Call is a mournful and soft 'wee-eet', not quite, but very nearly two syllables. The song is a beautiful, wistful, liquid cadence, starting quietly, then becoming clearer and more deliberate, descending to a distinctive flourish at the end, '— — hoo-eet, hoo-eet-oo'. On migration, the call note is usually the only sound to be heard, but occasionally a hint of the full song is given, enough to be immediately diagnostic.

SIMILAR SPECIES   Wood Warbler is larger with stronger contrast between yellow breast and white belly.

Bonelli's Warbler is generally a greyer bird and shows yellow on rump.

Melodious Warbler—may be confused with first-year Willow Warbler, but Melodious is larger, has a *Hippolais* head shape and bill and is a less delicate mover in the foliage.

Other *Phylloscopus* Warblers, apart from Chiffchaff, have obvious wingbars or distinctive supercilia or tail colouring.

Chiffchaff—usually has darker legs, more certainly in breeding season; noticeably shorter wings; usually looks less yellow below and less green above (in Europe). More usually confined to high tree tops and seldom descends to low bushes, where Willow Warbler may frequently occur. Whilst Willow Warblers song is immediately distinctive, the call is very similar to Chiffchaff's, but Chiffchaff's 'hoo-eet' is very definitely two syllables.

Goldcrest

PLATE 32

Regulus regulus (Linnaeus)

FH. Roitelet huppé   DU. Goudhaantje
IT. Regolo   GR. Wintergoldhähnchen
SW. Kungsfågel   SP. Reyezuelo

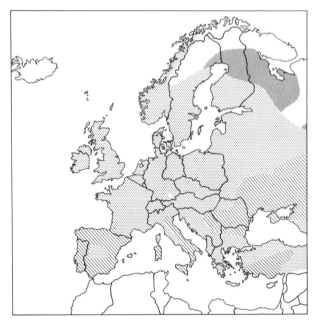

Breeding
Present in
summer only

Breeding
Present through-
out the year

Occurs in
winter

DISTRIBUTION AND HABITAT	Azores, Europe (north of the Pyrenees) and eastward discontinuously across Asia to Japan and central China. Migrates to southern part of breeding range, Mediterranean region, south Asia and south China, and there are limited local and altitudinal movements.

In the breeding season conifer (especially fir) woods, mixed woods and gardens with conifers. Also occasionally non-coniferous woodlands and thickets. After breeding and in winter more frequently deciduous trees, but also conifers and in hedgerows, thickets, and gardens.

DESCRIPTION
Length 3½ in (9 cm)

Upperparts and flanks dull greenish-yellow, brighter on rump and uppertail coverts. Forehead is dusky brown and the normally concealed crest has an orange centre, yellow in female. Sides of crown are black. Underparts are dusky white with a pale brown throat and shading to green on the flanks. Tail is dark brown with outer edges fringed yellowish-green. Wings are dark brown and show two white wingbars and a band of black. The male is generally paler on the upperparts than the female.

The immature is greyer than the adults and has no crest or crown colour except the black line at the crownsides. Underparts are paler than the adults'.

Bill and iris are very dark brown, and legs vary from pale to dark brown.

The geographical variation is clinal. From the British Isles, the populations become paler as they range eastwards across Europe into Asia. Also from southeastern Europe through the Caucasus to Iran they become duller and greyer.

IN THE FIELD   Very small, plump, compact bird, olive-green above and whitish below with a short tail and tiny bill. White wingbars often more noticeable than the coloured crest. Dark eye appears abnormally large and is surrounded by pale area, making this a most recognizable feature. Flight is tit-like with rapid wing beats and undulates when prolonged, but the bird prefers brief flits from tree to tree. Restless and active, often hanging tit-like from twigs, but generally behaves more like a warbler than a tit. Normally well up in trees, but on migration will use vegetation of any height. Flicks wings while feeding. Gregarious outside the breeding season in small parties or in flocks with tits.

SONG   Call is a very thin, high-pitched, shrill 'zeec, zeec, zeec'. The song consists of a soft and very high-pitched double note with a small trilling flourish near the end. In autumn the bird has a longer musical subsong of soft, rambling twittering, reminiscent of a Robin (*Erithacus rubecula*). The song is difficult to separate and is audible only over a short distance.

SIMILAR SPECIES   Strong and obvious similarity with the Firecrest, but see under that bird for differences.

Pallas' Leaf Warbler—has bright yellow rump band and yellow coronal stripe.

Yellow-browed Warbler—slightly larger, longer bill, more obviously *Phylloscopus* head shape, yellow superciliary stripe, and is slenderer and paler than immature Goldcrest.

Call note may be confused with Coal Tit (*Parus ater*) or Treecreeper (*Certhia familiaris*) but is higher pitched and less clearly audible.

Firecrest

PLATE 32

Regulus ignicapillus (Temminck)

FH. Roitelet à triple bandeau   DU. Vuurgoudhaantje
IT. Fiorrancino   GR. Sommergoldhähnchen
SW. Brandkronad kungsfågel   SP. Reyezuelo listado

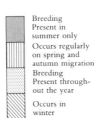

Breeding
Present in
summer only

Occurs regularly
on spring and
autumn migration

Breeding
Present through-
out the year

Occurs in
winter

DISTRIBUTION
AND HABITAT

Breeds in central and W. Europe from Denmark and S.W. Russia, south to Mediterranean area, Balkans and Asia Minor. Also breeds in N. Africa, Madeira, and Canary Is. Partially migratory, wintering south of the breeding range. Gradually extending its range northward where small numbers are regularly recorded with a few over-wintering.

Habitat is similar to Goldcrest's but is less restricted to conifers. Still mainly breeds in conifers or mixed woods, but also favours evergreen oak and alder swamps. After the breeding season may be found in almost any trees, coniferous or deciduous, but frequently occurs in ilex and cork oaks. Occasionally is found in low bushes, hedgerows, scrub, and dead bracken.

135

DESCRIPTION   Length 3½ in (9 cm)
Upperparts and flanks yellow-green. Head crest bright orange-red, yellow in female, bordered by two black stripes meeting on the forehead. Very prominent white supercilium with black stripe through the eye and white patch under it. Underparts pale dusky white, purer on belly. Bronzy gold patch on sides of neck and two strongly marked white wingbars.
Juvenile has faintly marked black and white stripes on head, but no crest. Flight feathers have no pale borders, but the double wingbar is still strongly marked. Underparts whiter than adult's.
Bill black. Legs and iris dark brown.

IN THE FIELD   Coloured like Goldcrest, but with greener upperparts contrasting with whiter underparts. White supercilium and black eye line immediately noticeable. Same restless behaviour and predilection for consorting with tits. Often found at lower levels than Goldcrest and consequently more easily studied.

SONG   Call is lower in pitch and less feeble than Goldcrest's. More audible and includes a characteristic 'zit–zit–zit'. The song is exactly similar to Goldcrest's but lacks the trilling flourish near the end, thus seeming to be more monotonous. Pitch somewhat lower than Goldcrest's but again stronger and more audible.

SIMILAR
SPECIES   Looks cleaner and sharper than Goldcrest, and Firecrest's supercilium is quite diagnostic. Lack of yellow rump distinguishes Firecrest from Pallas' Leaf Warbler.

References

Journal references not marked with species' names are of a general nature.

BOOKS

Ali, S. and Ripley, S. D. (1973) *Handbook of the birds of India and Pakistan*, Vol. 8. Bombay.
BOU (1971). *Status of birds in Britain and Ireland*. Blackwell, Oxford.
Brown, P. E. and Davies, M. G. (1949). *Reed warblers*. East Molesey.
Bruun, B. *et al.* (1970). *The Hamlyn guide to Birds of Britain and Europe*. Hamlyn, London.
Dementiev, G. P. *et al.* (1954). *Birds of the Soviet Union*. Moscow.
Etchécopar, R. D. and Hué, F. (1967). *Oiseaux du Nord de L'Afrique*. Paris.
Etchécopar, R. D. and Hué, F. (1978). *Oiseaux du Proche et du Moyen Orient*. Paris.
Heinzel, H. *et al.* (1972) *Birds of Britain and Europe*. Collins, London.
Hollom, P. A. D. (1980). *Popular handbook of rarer British birds,* 2nd. edn. Witherby, London.
Peterson, R. T. *et al.* (1954). *Field guide to the Birds of Britain and Europe*. Collins, London.
Sharrock, J. T. R. and Sharrock, E. M. (1976). *Rare birds in Britain and Ireland*. Berkhamstead.
Sharrock, J. T. R. (ed.) (1980). *Frontiers of bird identification*. Macmillan, London.
Snow, D. W. (1967). *A guide to moult in British birds*. Field Guide No. 11. BTO, Oxford.
Stresemann, E. and Portenko, L. A. (1960). *Atlas der Verbreitung palaearktischer Vögel*. Berlin.
Svensson, L. (1970). *Identification guide to European passerines*. Natur Riksmuseet, Stockholm.
Ticehurst, C. B. (1938). *A systematic review of the genus* Phylloscopus. British Museum (Natural History), London.
Vaurie, C. (1959). *The birds of the Palaearctic fauna*, Vol. I *Passeriformes*. Witherby, London.
Voous, K. (1960). *Atlas of European birds*. Nelson, London.
Williamson, K. (1960). *Identification for ringers*, Vol. 1 *Cettia* etc. BTO, Oxford.
Williamson, K. (1962). *Identification for ringers*, Vol. 2 *Phylloscopus*. BTO, Oxford.
Williamson, K. (1964). *Identification for ringers*, Vol. 3 *Sylvia*. BTO, Oxford.
Witherby, H. F. *et al.* (1938–41). *Handbook of British birds*. Witherby, London.

JOURNALS

Acklam, G. H. *et al.* (1956). *Br. Birds* **49,** 86.   Subalpine
Adams, M. C. (1980). *Br. Birds* **73,** 477.   Goldcrest/
                                                                           Firecrest

Alexander, H. G. (1955). *Br. Birds* **48,** 293.
Alexander, H. G. (1979). *Br. Birds* **72,** 130.   Yellow-browed

Reference	Species
Ash, J. (1956). *Br. Birds* **49**, 85.	Aquatic
Ash, J. S. (1960). *Br. Birds* **53**, 359.	Reed
Axell, H. E. (1955). *Br. Birds* **48**, 514.	Aquatic
Axell, H. E. (1958). *Br. Birds* **51**, 125.	Greenish
Axell, H. E. and Jobson, G. J. (1972). *Br. Birds* **65**, 229	Savi's
Barclay, M. and Pease, H. (1938). *Ibis* **81**, 144.	Sardinian/ Rüppell's
Beven, G. and England, M. D. (1967). *Br. Birds* **60**, 123.	Subalpine
Bibby, C. J. (1980). *Br. Birds* **73**, 367.	Moustached/ Sedge
Bonham, P. F. and Robertson, J. C. M. (1975). *Br. Birds* **68**, 393.	Cetti's
Boston, F. M. (1956). *Br. Birds* **49**, 326.	Savi's
Boswall, J. (1967). *Br. Birds* **60**, 523	Pallas' Grasshopper
Boswall, J. (1968). *Br. Birds* **61**, 34.	Blyth's Reed
Boswall, J. (1970). *Br. Birds* **63**, 255.	Radde's
Britton, D. *et al.* (1980). *Br. Birds* **73**, 589.	Blyth's Reed/ Paddyfield
Britton, D. J. (1980). *Br. Birds* **73**, 233.	Desert
Browne, P. W. P. (1952). *Br. Birds* **45**, 413.	Greenish
Browne, P. W. P. (1953). *Br. Birds* **46**, 456.	Greenish
Bryson, A. G. S. (1956). *Br. Birds* **49**, 43.	Greenish
Burton, J. F. (1979). *Br. Birds* **72**, 184.	Cetti's
Cade, M. (1980). *Br. Birds* **73**, 37.	Fantailed
Cantello, J. (1979). *Br. Birds* **72**, 483.	Dusky
Chapman, M. S. (1979). *Br. Birds* **72**, 437.	Booted
Christie, D. A. (1975). *Br. Birds* **68**, 176.	Barred
Clafton, F. R. (1968). *Br. Birds* **61**, 269.	Grasshopper/ Pallas' Grasshopper
Clafton, F. R. (1972). *Br. Birds* **65**, 460.	Desert
Clancey, P. A. (1950). *Br. Birds* **43**, 188.	Willow
Cobb, F. K. (1976). *Br. Birds* **69**, 447.	Goldcrest/ Firecrest
Conder, P. J. and Keighley, J. (1950). *Br. Birds* **43**, 238.	Willow/ Chiffchaff
Cudworth, J. (1979). *Br. Birds* **72**, 123.	Desert
da Prato, E. S. (1980). *Br. Birds* **73**, 315.	Sedge
Davis, P. (1958). *Br. Birds* **51**, 243.	Lanceolated
Davis, P. (1958). *Bull. FIBO* **4**, 127.	Arctic
Davis, P. (1959). *Br. Birds* **52**, 123.	Booted
Davis, P. (1960). *Br. Birds* **53**, 123.	Booted
Davis, P. (1961). *Br. Birds* **54**, 142.	Lanceolated
Davis, P. (1962). *Br. Birds* **55**, 137.	Dusky
Davis, P. (1962). *Br. Birds* **55**, 190.	River
Davis, P. (1965). *Br. Birds* **58**, 184.	Reed/Marsh
Densley, M. (1982). *Br. Birds* **75**, 133.	Pallas' Grasshopper

Dowsett-Lemaire, F. and Dowsett, R. J. (1979). *Br. Birds* **72,** 190. — Reed/Marsh

Ferguson-Lees, I. J. (1954). *Br. Birds* **47,** 121. — Icterine

Ferguson-Lees, I. J. and England, M. D. (1961). *Br. Birds* **54,** 395. — Bonelli's

Ferguson-Lees, I. J. (1964). *Br. Birds* **57,** 357. — Cetti's

Ferguson-Lees, I. J. (1967). *Br. Birds* **60,** 480. — Sardinian

Flumm, D. S. and Lord, N. A. G. (1978). *Br. Birds* **71,** 95. — Paddyfield

Fry, C. H. (1959). *Br. Birds* **52,** 20. — Orphean

Fry, C. H. *et al.* (1974). *Ibis* **116,** 340. — Blyth's Reed

Gantlett, S. J. M. (1979). *Br. Birds* **72,** 82. — *Hippolais* spp

Gaston, A. J. (1974). *Ibis* **116,** 432. — *Phylloscopus* spp

Gillham, E. H. and Holmes, R. C. (1952). *Br. Birds* **45,** 412. — Moustached

Graham Bell, D. (1979). *Br. Birds* **72,** 348. — Paddyfield

Grant, P. J. (1978). *Br. Birds* **71,** 132. — Icterine/Melodious

Grant, P. J. and Colston, P. R. (1979). *Br. Birds* **72,** 436. — *Hippolais* spp

Grant, P. J. (1980). *Br. Birds* **73,** 186. — Marsh/Blyth's Reed

Houston, I. and Robinson, (1951). *Br. Birds* **44,** 202. — Great Reed

Johns, R. J. and Wallace, D. I. M. (1972). *Br. Birds* **65,** 497. — Radde's/Dusky

Kitson, A. R. (1979). *Br. Birds* **72,** 6. — Desert

Kitson, A. R. (1979). *Br. Birds* **72,** 7. — Greenish/Green

Kitson, A. R. (1980). *Br. Birds* **73,** 398. — Paddyfield/Pallas' Grasshopper

Lassey, P. A. and Wallace, D. I. M. (1979). *Br. Birds* **72,** 82. — Dusky

Leisler, B. (1972). *J. Orn., Lpz.* **113,** 191. — Moustached

Lundevall, C. F. (1960). *Fauna Flora, Upps.* **48,** 229 — Greenish

Manns, D. J. (1979). *Br. Birds* **72,** 184. — Cetti's

Martins, R. P. (1981). *Br. Birds* **74,** 279. — Rüppell's

Mason, C. F. (1976). *Bird Study* **23,** 213. — *Sylvia* spp

McVail, M. J. and Smith, F. R. (1957). *Br. Birds* **50,** 124. — Melodious

Meek, E. R. (1978). *Br Birds* **71,** 464. — Yellow-browed

Meek, E. R. and Little, B. (1979). *Br. Birds* **72,** 353. — Paddyfield

Meiklejohn, M. F. M. and Reed, L. J. (1955). *Br. Birds* **48,** 514. — Aquatic

Mountfort, G. R. (1951). *Br. Birds* **44,** 195. — Great Reed

Neufeldt, I. (1960). *Br. Birds* **53,** 117. — Radde's

Neufeldt, I. (1967). *Br. Birds* **60,** 239. — Thick-billed

Nisbet, I. C. T. and Smout, T. C. (1957). *Br. Birds* **50,** 203. — Olivaceous

Nisbet, I. C. T. (1967). *Bird Study* **14,** 96. — Pallas' Grasshopper

Parker, S. A. and Harrison, C. J. O. (1963). *Bull. BOC* — Moustached

Pearson, D. J. *et al.* (1962). *Br. Birds* **55,** 277. — Bonelli's

Pearson, D. J. (1973). *Bird Study* **20,** 24. — Reed/Sedge/Garden/Willow

Pearson, D. J. (1981). *Br. Birds* **74,** 445. — Marsh/Reed

Pearson, R. (1979). *Ringing Migration* **2,** 156. — Willow

Pimm, S. L. (1973). *Condor* **75**, 386.   Whitethroat
Pitt, R. G. (1967). *Br. Birds* **60**, 349.   Savi's
Portenko, L. A. (1938). *Bull. Acad. Sci. URSS* 1051.   Arctic
Price, M. P. (1969). *Bird Study* **16**, 130.   Reed/Marsh
Quinn, A. and Clement, P. (1979). *Br. Birds* **72**, 484.   Yellow-browed
Reynolds, R. A. W. (1952). *Br. Birds* **45**, 220.   Great Reed
Rogers, M. J. (1968). *Br. Birds* **61**, 230.   Fan-tailed
Ruttledge, R. F. (1979). *Br. Birds* **72**, 129.   Blackcap
Salomonsen, F. (1929). *J. Orn. Eng. Bd.* **II**, 267.   Great Reed
Salomonsen, F. (1945). *Ark. Zool.* **36, 1**.   Willow
Scott, R. E. (1964). *Br. Birds* **57**, 508.   Pallas' Leaf
Scott, R. E. (1979). *Br. Birds* **72**, 124.   Yellow-browed
Sharrock , J. T. R. (1962). *Br. Birds* **55**, 90.   Sardinian/
                                                                             Subalpine/
                                                                             Spectacled

Sharrock, J. T. R. *et al.* (1970). *Br. Birds* **63**, 214.   Blyth's Reed
Sharrock, J. T. R. (1972). *Br. Birds* **65**, 501.   Fan-tailed
Sharrock, J. T. R. (1979). *Br. Birds* **72**, 596.   Blyth's Reed/
                                                                             Paddyfield
Sharrock, J. T. R. (1980). *Br. Birds* **73**, 158.   Yellow-browed
Sharrock, J. T. R. (1982). *Br. Birds* **75**, 86.   Barred
Shrubb, M. (1979). *Br. Birds* **72**, 485.   Yellow-browed
Simmons, K. E. L. (1951) *Ibis* **94**, 303.   Olivaceous
Smith, D. A. (1979). *Br. Birds* **72**, 387.   Booted
Smith, G. (1980). *Br. Birds.* **73**, 417.   Pallas'
                                                                           Grasshopper
Smout, T. C. (1960). *Br. Birds* **53**, 225.   Icterine
Stresemann, E. and Arnold, J. (1949). *J. Bombay nat. Hist.*   Great Reed/
  Soc. **48**, 428.   Clamorous
Stresemann, E. and Stresemann, V. (1970). *J. Orn., Lpz.*
  111, 237.   Savi's
Swanberg. P. O. and McNeile, J. H. (1948). *Br. Birds* **41**,
  330.   Arctic
Swift, J. J. (1959). *Br. Birds* **52**, 198.   Spectacled/
                                                                             Subalpine
Thearle, R. (1954). *Br. Birds* **47**, 408.   Greenish
Thearle, R. (1955). *Br. Birds* **48**, 284.   Melodious
Thearle, R. (1956). *Br. Birds* **49**, 232. (Also note by I. J.
  Ferguson-Lees.)   Melodious
Thielke, G., and Linsenmair, K. E. (1963). *J. Orn., Lpz.* **104**,   Willow/
  372.   Chiffchaff
Thomas, D. K. (1979). *Ringing Migration* **2**, 118.   Fan-tailed
Thorpe, W. H. (1957). *Br. Birds* **50**, 169.   Grasshopper/
                                                                             Savi's/River
Välikangas, I. (1951). *Ornis fenn.* **28**, 25.   Greenish
van der Dol, J. H. *et al.* (1979). *Br. Birds* **72**, 482.   Dusky
Vaurie, C. (1954). *Am. Mus. Novit.* 1685, 1691, 1692.
Vaurie, C. (1955). *Am. Mus. Novit.* 1753.
Wallace, D. I. M. (1964). *Br. Birds* **57**, 282.   *Hippolais* spp

Wallace, D. I. M. (1972). *Br. Birds* **65**, 170.   Booted
Wallace, D. I. M. (1973). *Br. Birds* **66**, 382.   Great Reed/
    Clamorous
Wallace, D. I. M. (1973). *Br. Birds* **66**, 385.   Blyth's Reed
Wallace, D. I. M. (1973). *Br. Birds* **66**, 386.   Lesser
    Whitethroat
Wallace, D. I. M. (1973). *Br. Birds* **66**, 388.   Yellow-browed
Warburg, G. and Warmington, E. H. (1956). *Br. Birds* **49**,
327.   Aquatic
Watson, G. E. (1962). *Ibis* **104**, 347.   Chiffchaff
Whitaker, B. (1955) *Br. Birds* **48**, 285.   Bonelli's
Whitaker, B. (1955). *Br. Birds* **48**, 515.   Sardinian
Williamson, K. (1950). *Br. Birds* **43**, 49.   Pallas'
    Grasshopper
Williamson, K. (1951). *Br. Birds* **44**, 147.   Yellow-browed/
    Arctic/Greenish
Williamson, K. (1951). *Scott. Nat.* **62**, 18.   Greenish
Williamson, K. (1954). *Br. Birds* **47**, 49.   Chiffchaff
Williamson, K. (1954). *Br. Birds* **47**, 297.   Paddyfield
Williamson, K. (1955). *Br. Birds* **48**, 561.   Chiffchaff
Williamson, K. (1956). *Br. Birds* **49**, 94.   Melodious
Williamson, K. *et al.* (1956). *Br. Birds* **49**, 89.   Thick-billed
Williamson, K. (1956). *Br. Birds* **49**, 119.   Icterine
Williamson, K. (1957). *Br. Birds* **50**, 395.   Pallas'
    Grasshopper
Wooldridge, G. E. and Ballantyne, C. B. (1952). *Br. Birds* **45**,
219.   Moustached
Zahavi, A. (1957). *Ibis* **99**, 600.   Great Reed/
    Clamorous

SOUND RECORDINGS

Lewis, V. Bird recognition: an aural index. HMV, London.
North, M. E. W. and Simms, E. Witherby's sound guide to British Birds.
  Witherby, London.
Palmer, S. and Boswall, J. Field guide to the songs of Britain and Europe. Sveriges
  Radio, Stockholm.
Reisinger, H. Die Singvögel Europas. Kosmos, Stuttgart.
Roché, J. C. A sound guide to the birds of Europe (3 Vols.) Int. Centre for Orn.
  Sound Pubs, Aubenas-les-Alpes, France.

Index

Page numbers for the main descriptions are given in **bold type**